MW00810521

BRANDING DEMOCRATS

Publishing

www.amplifypublishinggroup.com

Branding Democrats:
A Top-to-Bottom Reimagining of Campaign Strategies

For more information, please contact:
RealClear Publishing, an imprint of Amplify Publishing Group
620 Herndon Parkway, Suite 320
Herndon, VA 20170
info@amplifypublishing.com

Library of Congress Control Number: 2022900148

CPSIA Code: PRV0522A

ISBN-13: 978-1-63755-471-5

Printed in the United States

Dedicated to the tens of thousands of poll workers and volunteer campaign staff who keep democracy alive in America.

BRANDING
DEMOCRATS

A TOP-TO-BOTTOM REIMAGINING

OF CAMPAIGN STRATEGIES

KEN WEBER   DARYL WEBER

RealClear
Publishing

CONTENTS

"He who moulds public sentiment goes deeper than he who enacts statutes or pronounces decisions."

—Abraham Lincoln, 1858

INTRODUCTION

The headline of the *Los Angeles Times* on July 7, 2021, was blunt: "Democrats brace for 2022 elections with 'little margin for error.'"

The article begins ominously: "Democrats are at high risk of losing control of Congress next year, and the perilous outlook is shaping party strategy on every level, a modern illustration of the old saw: Nothing focuses the mind like the sight of the gallows."*

"Little margin for error" is starkly realistic for two reasons: First, during most midterm elections, the party in power loses congressional seats.

---

* Janet Hook, "Democrats Brace for 2022 Elections with 'Little Margin for Error'," *Los Angeles Times*, June 7, 2021. https://www.latimes.com/politics/story/2021-06-07/democrats-brace-for-2022-elections-with-little-margin-for-error

And second, the 2020 elections gave Democrats a razor-thin majority in the House of Representatives and a tie in the Senate, meaning, in reality, there is no room for error.

Then there's this dark headline from Judd Legum's *Popular Information* newsletter on July 15, 2021: "How corporations give Republicans a massive financial advantage in state politics." And that story begins with:

> Over the last decade, public corporations have given Republicans at the state level a financial advantage that exceeds $200 million, according to new research provided exclusively to *Popular Information* by the Center for Political Accountability.*

Despite winning the House, Senate, and the White House in 2020, we on the Left must face up to a sad fact: there's very little good news for Democrats on the horizon. There is no question that the need for Democrats to do better is urgent—extremely urgent. Republicans have tacked sharply to the right. Many in top positions are aggressively pandering to the radical Right while compromising their ethics and values. And some of them are borderline crazy.

---

* Judd Legum, "How Corporations Give Republicans a Massive Financial Advantage in State Politics," n.d., https://popular.info/p/how-corporations-give-republicans.

We can't dawdle. America's future depends on Democrats doing better in elections.

After every election, pundits tell us *why Democrats should have done better*. They lay out their reasons, and most present smart, insightful examinations of what happened in *this* particular election.

This is fine, but it misses the larger point.

Democrats fail to achieve widespread and sustained election success because they fail to exploit the tenets of *long-term* branding and smart marketing.

This book is a handbook—a field guide for every Democratic candidate and those who support them at every level, from the smallest local elections to national offices. The techniques are roughly the same for every candidate.

We all know that a huge percentage of Americans rarely, if ever, read a respected newspaper or watch network news shows. They don't subscribe to quality news magazines or listen to news-related podcasts or radio.

Worse, few, if they care about the news at all, get their information from accredited, reliable media sources. They have trouble naming even one of their senators, let alone their congressional representative. And they certainly cannot name the person who represents them on their city council or county board. So when they walk into a voting booth, they may have some idea of who's at the top of the ticket. But as they go down the ballot, they are looking at names that might as well be in Serbo-Croatian.

That's why long-term branding is vital.

If you yourself are a Democratic politician, it's reasonable to assume you are fairly smart, articulate, and passionate about the important issues of the day.

But none of that means you have any experience with or insight into branding and marketing. You might say, "Hey, we have consultants who do all that." To which we say yes, but if they had been better at their jobs there would be no need for us to write this book. Democrats would be winning more of the close elections.

This sad phenomenon is real. Here's a story from the *New York Times*, published on February 21, 2021:

> **"Democrats Beat Trump in 2020. Now They're Asking: What Went Wrong?"**
> In the past, Democratic attempts at self-scrutiny have tended to yield somewhat mushy conclusions aimed at avoiding controversy across the party's multifarious coalition.*

---

* Alexander Burns, "Democrats Beat Trump in 2020. Now They're Asking: What Went Wrong?," *New York Times*, February 20, 2021, https://www.nytimes.com/2021/02/20/us/politics/democrats-house-races-trump.html.

Indeed. But smart branding sidesteps "mushy conclusions." It can apply to every candidate and every campaign.

Our goal here is nothing less than a major reset, a rejection of most traditional Democratic marketing strategies.

We're going to present you with new techniques for reframing old strategies.

Our target in the following pages is the 1 or 2 percent—the small slice of the electorate that frequently shifts elections from red to blue, or vice versa. And we want to motivate the "surge" voters, those who lean to the left but tend to wait for the "critical" presidential elections. We want them to vote in every election.

Plus, there is an even bigger opportunity for Democrats to reach the huge portion of the electorate that doesn't vote at all. Gen Z especially is just starting to form political opinions, and they can become lifelong Democrats if we reach them with effective messaging.

And then there's this often overlooked fact: today's fourteen- and fifteen-year-olds are only two election cycles away from getting a ballot! They are far more comfortable with LGBTQ, racial, and environmental issues than earlier generations. Importantly, they would seem to have a natural affinity for the Democratic brand. According to the Pew Research Center ("On the Cusp of Adulthood and Facing an Uncertain Future: What We Know About Gen Z So Far"):

"[A]mong Americans ages 13 and older (the survey was done in the fall of 2018) found that, similar to Millennials, Gen Zers are progressive and pro-government, most see the country's growing racial and ethnic diversity as a good thing, and they're less likely than older generations to see the United States as superior to other nations." These young voters need to be brought into the fold as quickly as possible.

We must start "cultivating" everyone, and we need to do it now.

If you are a seasoned political player, you might think you already know how to campaign and message. But as we point out again and again, past branding and marketing mistakes by Democrats at every level of politics have yielded less-than-ideal results.

This book is a compendium of needed actions. They have never been collected in one place before, and we are certain you have not previously seen many of these suggestions.

Democrats cannot and do not need to win over vast swaths of hard-line conservative voters. Most Americans are immutable when it comes to party affiliation. But if the suggestions here can move that 1 or 2 percent toward our team, that might be enough to push an election—and the future of our country—in the right direction.

On July 25, 2021, Rahm Emanuel correctly pointed out on ABC's *This Week with George Stephanopoulos*:

"The election will be won in swing states by swing voters in swing districts."

Let's get those swing voters. We can—with smart branding and marketing techniques.

Republicans Are Moving Quickly to Restrict Voting Rights

Donald Trump's Big Lie about voter fraud has a vice-grip on the Grand Old Party. From the moment it became clear that Joe Biden won the 2020 presidential election, Republican lawmakers sprang into action, and GOP state legislators introduced hundreds of bills across the country designed to restrict voting access.

According to the nonpartisan Brennan Center for Justice, the assault on voting rights began early in 2021, with the introduction of 253 bills proposing voting restrictions across forty-three states as of mid-February 2021. That's a horrendous situation, but it quickly became worse. As of mid-May 2021, that number rose to at least 389 bills in forty-eight states.

And no one is fooled: all these bills purporting to "secure election integrity" are thinly veiled efforts to make it harder for voters in traditionally Democratic areas to cast their votes.

We know most of the proposed bills will fail, but enough

have already passed—and will pass—to make the coming elections even more of an uphill climb for Democrats. By some measures it's already too late. With roughly half of all state governments currently under Republican control, the impact on tens of millions of voters could be dramatic, widening a stark geographic divide in ballot access.

For these and so many other reasons, the need for Democrats to retool their campaign strategies becomes more critical by the minute.

How Will This Book Help Save the Democratic Party from Itself?

We'll lay out a process to reinvigorate the Democratic brand to give every candidate at every level—from local to state to national—a head start in winning their election. And we'll examine some notable case studies of failing Democratic campaigns of the past.

We'll show you how to reposition Democrats as the party that "fights for the people," how to make the branding personal, and how to claim the upper hand in differentiating Democratic policies from the Republican policies of pandering to corporations and the wealthiest Americans.

We'll put forward a plan to build the base, reinforce the brand in a positive and persistent manner, and inject a greater sense of confidence in touting the accomplishments and positive attributes of the Democratic Party.

We must start "cultivating" everyone, and we need to do it as soon as possible.

If you are a seasoned political player, you already know some or much of what you will read in these pages. But as we point out again and again, past branding and marketing mistakes by Democrats at every level of politics have yielded less-than-ideal results.

In short, we put forward methods and strategies to change the way the public views the Democratic Party.

Who Is This For?

This book, which began as a five-page online article, was initially aimed at the most visible Democrats—those holding or running for a seat in Congress. But as we expanded upon and explained in greater detail our branding and marketing techniques, it soon became obvious that our expertise in and knowledge of these techniques would be invaluable for Democratic politicians at every level.

This book is for those running for office, those in office, the folks on their campaign staff, and anyone, anywhere—from the most motivated activists to the average citizen—who can help Democrats win.

This book will not be particularly helpful for Democrats battling other Democrats in primaries, although much of our advice applies to campaigning in general. Rather, we hope Democrats will use the ammunition herein to vanquish Republicans.

And finally, we realized this would be useful knowledge for any person considering taking a shot at joining the political circus—local, state, or national. Reading this might help those people decide if they are ready to toss their hat into the ring. (We hope you do!)

Who Are You Guys?

Ken Weber and Daryl Weber have established successful careers utilizing the innovative and effective brand building and long-term marketing strategies they share in this book. Both are passionate about politics in general and Democratic politics specifically, and they firmly believe the party could achieve continuing success well beyond a single election cycle by implementing a consistent, comprehensive marketing and branding strategy.

Ken Weber, the author of *Dear Investor, What the HELL are You Doing?*, started an investment advisory business thirty years ago. Through innovative marketing and branding, he built it into one of the top 10 percent of investment advisories nationwide, based on assets under management.

Daryl Weber, Ken's son, is the author of *Brand Seduction: How Neuroscience Can Help Marketers Build Memorable Brands*, which has been translated into several languages and has received rave industry reviews. A graduate of Columbia University, Daryl has worked as a brand strategist for some of the biggest brands in the world, including Coca-Cola, Nike, Johnnie Walker, Google, and many others. He was previously global director of creative strategy at the Coca-Cola Company and a strategy director at the brand consulting firm Redscout. Marketing guru Seth Godin has called *Brand Seduction* "powerful, profound, and beautifully written. *Brand Seduction* raises the bar for every marketer to do work that truly matters."

Their advice in these pages is based on hundreds of hours of conversation and yelling at the television screen—that would be Ken—when Democrats do dumb things.

CHAPTER 1

DEMOCRATS ARE TERRIBLE AT BRANDING

Yes, they are. We'll carefully break down their branding failures in the following pages. But first some definitions.

Branding is not *marketing*. Marketing deals with specifics and seeks immediate response. For example, "Our watches are on sale this week; buy our watches."

Branding describes how you think and *feel* about something—a product, a service, a candidate, a political party. Branding is for the long term—"Rolex watches tell the world you are successful." They make you feel good about yourself.

In practical terms, a Rolex is no more accurate than any other modern watch, and many other companies produce equally attractive watches. But thanks to decades of smart branding, people are willing to pay a big premium for that Rolex on their wrist.

Rolex frequently takes out full-page ads in major newspapers. Do you know what is rarely mentioned? The watch! The ads are purely for branding. They are meant to trigger emotions—feelings of success, glamour, visibility.

Fox News can also teach us about branding. They came out of nowhere and immediately called themselves, with audacious chutzpah, "America's Newsroom." More importantly, they pounded the message "Fair and Balanced" into the consciousness of every viewer. And although they dropped that—now farcical—phrase years ago, it still reverberates across the media landscape. It was a branding coup.

Branding, unlike marketing, is for the long run. In a nutshell, that is the animating thesis of this book. We urge Democrats to think far beyond the next election cycle. By improving branding for the long term, short-term results will likely improve as well.

Branding is the bedrock of most successful companies. Surely these taglines are familiar to you:

- The Ultimate Driving Machine
- The Best a Man Can Get
- A Diamond Is Forever
- You're in Good Hands

- Finger-Lickin' Good
- 15 minutes could save you 15 percent or more on car insurance.

BMW, Gillette, De Beers, Allstate, KFC, GEICO. Each tagline has been around for decades, and each, in a tiny number of words, encapsulates its product or service with specificity. None of these taglines changed to meet quarterly goals or yearly targets. They were all designed to stick inside consumers' brains—and thanks to endless repetition, they do.

Branding, thoughtfully devised and used continuously, works for businesses. It surely works for political parties and their candidates as well. In political terms, marketing (or *advertising* or *messaging*) targets *current* issues. Arguments about tax rates, trade policy with China, immigration issues, and so on are all fodder for political marketing.

Branding, however, goes to how voters perceive parties and their candidates. More broadly, political branding seeks to influence how voters *feel* about parties and their candidates, apart from the current menu of topics in today's news.

Political *marketing* is: Candidate Joe Smith wants the federal government to be allowed to negotiate drug prices for Medicare.

Conversely, political *branding* is: Democrats fight for health care you can afford.

Political branding is far more important than political marketing, but we will touch on both in later sections.

Here's one thing we know for sure: Republicans are much better at branding than Democrats.

We Democrats need to fix that, and we need to do it immediately.

Our Branding Is Broken

The Democrats' branding problem has been brewing for decades. Barack Obama won the presidency in 2008 by being the "change" candidate, but two years later, in the midterm elections, he let his party get "shellacked" (his word) because *he let Republicans set the narrative*. Obama and most Democrats failed to assertively remind voters that Republicans badly messed up the economy, and Democrats fixed it.

This was inexcusable.

Recall the situation in 2010: George W. Bush and his Republican administration left office having put our nation into two disastrous wars based on false information. Unemployment was soaring, the stock market was in a free fall, and fear was rampant. And, of course, the worst terrorist attack on American soil happened under their watch. By any rational standard that horrendous Republican track record should have handed Democrats massive wins for many years into the future.

But it didn't.

What happened in 2010 must be seen as an historic political failure. A mere two years after the worst economic meltdown since the Great Depression, Democrats let the GOP walk all over them.

There is no stronger example of how terrible Democrats are at branding.

Worse still, that fiasco was not an isolated incident. In 2020 Joe Biden ran against an *impeached* president with unemployment soaring and a deadly pandemic raging. While Biden's 306 electoral votes and his 7-million-vote margin in the popular vote made it seem like a substantial win, he in fact won thanks to narrow victories in just three swing states.

If Donald Trump had garnered the right mix of 42,921 votes in Arizona (10,457), Georgia (11,779), and Wisconsin (20,682), the Electoral College would have tied at 269.

Just 43,000 votes out of more than 155 million! That incredibly tiny number is all that was needed to flip the 2020 election to Trump. When candidates end up tied in the Electoral College, the decision goes to the House. But each state gets only one vote for president, so Trump would have won.

With an Electoral College victory that close, the only obvious conclusion must be: if Trump had not bungled the COVID-19 crisis as badly as he did, he likely would have won. To think otherwise is foolish.

And if that wasn't bad enough, Trump *increased* his vote tally from 2016! He even improved his results among minorities!

Aside from Biden's narrow victory, the down-ballot races for Democrats were a disaster. Despite the many polls predicting a powerful "blue wave," all we got was a limp blue drip. Dems gained a mere three new seats in the Senate—thanks in large part to the heroic efforts of Stacey Abrams and other activists—but in the House their majority shrank from thirty-five seats all the way down to a slim four-seat margin!

Results for Democrats in 2020 were equally bad, or worse, in state and local elections.

Obama's problems in 2010 were pervasive throughout the Democratic party. Then we saw many of the same problems a decade later. So yes, absolutely, our branding is broken.

The NBC News website on November 22, 2020, spoke of our "deeper problems":

> **"'A huge catastrophe': Democrats grapple with congressional and state election losses."***

Biden's win obscures deeper problems that have left the

---

* Alex Seitz-Wald and Benjy Sarlin, "'A Huge Catastrophe': Democrats Grapple with Congressional and State Election Losses," NBC News, November 22, 2020, https://www.nbcnews.com/politics/2020-election/huge-catastrophe-democrats-grapple-congressional-state-election-losses-n1248529.

party with an uncertain future. Over the course of more than ten years, nothing has changed. Democrats never seem to learn.

Democrats cannot afford "an uncertain future."

This country is on a precipice, and if we don't change our approach to campaigning, it might become too late.

We're going to "Define the Brand" in the next chapter. But first we want you to acknowledge this hard truth:

Democrats Make Every Candidate Start from Zero

Each candidate runs his or her own campaign as if there were no history, no follow-through from previous campaigns.

That is their most basic branding mistake:
Democratic branding is nonexistent.

In just about every campaign, Democrats try to focus on "local issues" or current issues, but they neglect to build a larger, overarching message.

Each candidate's ads say nice things about her or him. Or, even more often, they run ads saying nasty things about their opponent. Frequently, they try to "play to the middle" by being part Republican, part Democrat.

Contrast that with, say, Bernie Sanders. He's a disheveled,

cranky old man. Yet he pounded the same few highly focused issues over and over, and millions responded with powerful enthusiasm. He has always spoken—and still does—with full-throated passion, and he still wins all his Senate elections easily. And despite his "Democratic Socialist" label, he vanquished his stage-filling army of opponents, save one, in the 2020 primaries.

Trump, too, understood branding. He never strayed far from his few key issues: "Make America Great Again." "Drain the swamp." "Cut taxes." "Strengthen the military." "China is stealing jobs from us." His three biggest campaign promises—"We'll build the wall, and Mexico will pay for it"; "Repeal and replace Obamacare with something terrific"; and "I'll show my taxes after the election"—were never fulfilled. Yet his 2020 campaign slogan was "Promises made. Promises kept." And they sold it!

In 2016 Hillary Clinton floundered, even though, under her predecessor (Obama), the economy enjoyed one of the most robust economic recoveries in US history. Unemployment dropped by more than 50 percent, economic growth rebounded sharply, and stocks surged nearly 200 percent. But there was virtually no mention of this historic resurgence in the Hillary campaign. It could have been: "We're the party of economic growth." "We're the party of full employment." "We're the party that tripled your money in the stock market." But the Democratic Party—from the top of the ticket to the state and local races—seemed totally unaware of the economic miracle that their party had just engineered.

In 2016 and again in 2020, it seemed all the down-ticket Democrats were on their own, desperately trying to craft their own messaging. The answer must be this: *stop making every candidate reinvent the wheel!*

All Democratic candidates and elected officials need to send the same message, and they do that by saying the same words and phrases. They need to say them over and over. All of us, whether in office, running for office, party workers, or just citizens who want to affect change, need to get on board and stay on board with the Democratic brand.

Remember, most people vote by party first, not by the candidate. But Democrats almost always focus on building up the person rather than the party. That's a massive mistake.

Instead, we must build the overall Democratic brand.

And we need to start immediately.

Republicans Beat Us by Staying on Message

Perhaps it's the continuing influence of Frank Luntz or Roger Ailes or someone else. But for whatever reason, Republicans come up with highly effective catchphrases, and they repeat them not for a few days or weeks but for years. Decades even.

Look at some of the phrases the Right has permanently ingrained into our collective consciousness.

First the negative slogans used by Republicans against Democrats:

1. Socialists
2. Tax-and-spend liberals
3. Liberal media
4. Soft on crime
5. Coastal elites (or just "elites")
6. The nanny state
7. Death tax
8. Job-killing taxes
9. Job-killing regulations
10. Government takeover of health care
11. Socialized medicine
12. Fake news (We used that phrase first because of *actual* fake news.)
13. The war on Christmas
14. Open borders
15. Massive voter fraud
16. Government handouts
17. Partial-birth abortion
18. Cancel culture
19. Radical Left agenda
20. Deep state

Every voter knows those words, none of which accurately reflect political reality. Republicans have successfully pounded Democrats with these words for years.

It's bumper-sticker politics. No idea that needs a second paragraph for nuance or explanation makes it into Republican policy. But it's been effective for decades.

On the flip side, what are the negative "branding" words

and phrases Democrats use against Republicans?

1. _____

2. _____

3. _____

Right. There aren't any. Zero. (You might point to the "Big Lie" about voter fraud, which is potent, but likely won't have staying power.)

This is a terrible state of affairs for our team.

But we can change that. We will show how later on.

And then there are the *positive* words and phrases that Republicans have successfully appropriated as their own, again with little or no basis in reality:

1. Family values
2. Job creators and wealth creators
3. Military strength
4. Fiscal responsibility
5. Pro-business
6. Law and order
7. Gun rights
8. Secure borders
9. America first
10. Pro-life
11. Freedom
12. Personal responsibility
13. Patriotism

Republicans own those phrases *because we let them*.

Worse, they repeat these phrases so often that even some Democrats end up using them in ways that backfire, which further solidifies these Republican framings in the minds of voters.

It's time to claw back the good words and counter the bad.

Case Study: Ossoff in 2017

Look at an example from the not-too-distant past. He's a senator now, but back when Jon Ossoff first ran for a congressional seat in 2017, he lost. In a *Washington Post* postelection article, he talked about the issues he brought into the campaign. The *first one* he mentioned was "I focused on the development of metro Atlanta into a world-class commercial capital."*

Great, but that's neither personal nor immediate.

Worse, *it is the same message any Republican could say*! Where was his brand? What was his overarching, deep-seated, deeply felt emotional theme?

And what was his connection back to Democratic principles? What was his connection to the Democrat brand?

---

* Jon Ossoff, "Jon Ossoff: Lessons for Democrats from the Georgia Election," editorial, *Washington Post*, June 16, 2017, https://www.washingtonpost.com/opinions/jon-ossoff-what-democrats-won-in-georgia/2017/06/26/0f097992-5a84-11e7-9fc6-c7ef4bc58d13_story.html.

There was none.

The vast number of voters who don't keep up with the news won't fully grasp or visualize the "development of metro Atlanta into a world-class commercial capital."

Every voter and every human listens to the station WIIFM— What's in It for Me? The average working Jane or Joe can't easily relate to a "commercial capital" many years down the road. They want this morning's kitchen-table issues solved by their politicians.

Ossoff, in that congressional campaign, strayed from any Democratic brand message, just as Obama did in 2010. Just as so many Democrats do every election.

The lesson should not be lost on anyone: being a lone-wolf candidate, unmoored to a strong political brand, too often becomes a losing strategy.

We'll have lots more to say about all that shortly.

We Must Act Now

Every day that passes is a day Democrats are falling behind. Bluntly, we do not have time to waste.

According to the *New York Times*, January 31, 2021: "Some election experts believe the GOP could retake the house in

2022 based solely on gains from newly drawn districts."*

That's a frightening prospect. Yet a December 2020 Gallup poll found that 31 percent of Americans identified as Democrat, 25 percent identified as Republican, and 41 percent as Independent.†

By those metrics, it's reasonable to assume we should continually be controlling the three branches of the federal government and most state houses and legislature.

But we don't.

Yet.

*   Reid J Epstein and Nick Corasaniti, "The Gerrymander Battles Loom, as G.O.P. Looks to Press Its Advantage," *New York Times,* January 31, 2021, https://www. nytimes.com/2021/01/31/us/politics/gerrymander-census-democrats-republicans. html.

†   "Party Affiliation," Gallup, December 2020, https://news.gallup.com/poll/15370/party-affiliation.aspx.

Chapter 1 Summary

- Branding is the long-term feeling you have toward something. Marketing is the short-term play for sales or votes.

- Our branding is broken. Democrats have not clearly articulated what the Democrat brand overall stands for in citizens' minds.

- Democrats make every candidate start from zero. We have not created an overarching brand halo that every candidate can leverage, so every candidate starts from scratch.

- Republicans beat us by staying on message better than we do. They own the positive phrases that work for them as well as the negative ones they use against us.

- Ossoff in 2017 was a perfect case study of what we do wrong—he pushed local "rational" messages rather than a powerful emotional message that resonated.

- Almost every Democratic defeat in the last half century is a consequence of the party's failure to successfully create and deploy a national brand identity.

- We must change this, and we must do so quickly.

BUILDING THE DEMOCRATIC BRAND

Democrats should be cruising to victory far more frequently than they do.

Why? Because polls show that a majority of Americans agree with Democrats on most major issues! That's not partisan wishful thinking. A CNN.com headline from April 7, 2019, told us,

"The majority of Americans tend to agree with Democrats on top issues, polling shows."* The story was based on a wide-ranging Gallup poll.

---

* Grace Sparks, "The Majority of Americans Tend to Agree with Democrats on Top Issues, Polling Shows," CNN (Cable News Network, April 7, 2019), https://www.cnn.com/2019/04/07/politics/democratic-positions-majority/index.html.

Consider the issues most Democrats stand for:

- Protect Social Security (we invented it)
- Protect Medicare and Medicaid (we invented them)
- Rational gun safety laws
- Protect the environment
- Support Planned Parenthood and similar organizations
- Women's rights
- Minority rights
- Workers' rights and protections
- LGBTQ rights
- Equal pay for equal work
- Safe abortion availability
- Reliable and safe roads, tunnels, and bridges
- A fair tax system that reduces inequality
- Higher minimum wage
- Affordable health care for all
- Quality education for all
- Support for veterans
- A pro-growth business environment that produces safe, satisfying, well-paying jobs
- Fair and open elections
- Access to reliable internet
- Fair and compassionate immigration policies

Notice that none of these bullet points relate to anything like building the "commercial capital" Jon Ossoff spoke about. Nor are these fringe or radical issues. These are the breakfast-table issues on which most Americans agree.

Want more evidence? Here's a poll published by the Pew Research Center, May 17, 2021, to back us up[*]:

Percentage of Americans who say the federal government has a responsibility to provide _____ for all Americans:

Clean air and water	87%
High-quality K-12 education	79%
Health Insurance	64%
Adequate income in retirement	58%
An adequate standard of living	56%
Access to high-speed internet	43%
A college education	39%

(A note about the 43 percent who want the federal government to help provide access to high-speed internet. You have to believe that that number is going to rise every year as fast internet access increasingly becomes a necessity of modern life.)

---

[*] "Americans See Broad Responsibilities for Government; Little Change Since 2019," Pew Research Center, May 17, 2021, https://www.pewresearch.org/politics/2021/05/17/americans-see-broad-responsibilities-for-government-little-change-since-2019/.

Clearly, as the polls show, Americans align with Democrats on the vital issues we all face. If all that is true—and it is—we Democrats control the high ground. So how can we possibly lose, and lose so badly, in hundreds of races? Because, as a party, we continually fail to develop smart branding.

Branding Must Feel Personal

Former Speaker of the House Tip O'Neill famously said, "All politics is local." That phrase has hurt Democrats. Too many times Democrats tried to be "local," and as a result they lost their moorings as Democrats. They strayed from the brand.

O'Neill was right. All politics is local—potholes, schools, business, and farm policy, etc.—but only *after* the campaign.

During the campaign all politics is *personal*.

How does each voter see him or herself? They see themselves through their own personal lens:

- I am old.
- I am a parent.
- I am a student.
- I run a business.
- I am a Christian/Jew/ Muslim.

- I support Israel.
- I am worried about the future.
- I am sick.
- My children need help.
- I am a veteran.

- My parents are ill.
- I don't feel safe.
- Will I be able to retire?
- I depend on Social Security and Medicare.

We need to reach people through the personal concerns they feel in everyday life. Democrats like to be fact-based and logical. This is good, but it doesn't reach voters on an emotional level.

On the other hand, Republicans go right for your gut.

All marketers and branding experts know that emotions eclipse facts and logic, and Republicans exploit that fact instinctively and repeatedly. To play on our fears, they ominously warn us:

- Immigrants are dangerous.
- Crime on the streets is here (or coming).
- You need guns to protect yourself.
- Taxes will wipe out your savings.
- Gangs are coming for you.

Or they evoke our sense of personal responsibility:

- No free lunch.
- I worked hard, so you must too.
- I paid for college, and you have to do the same.

These Republican messages are personal and emotional, and many conjure up powerful images that stick. Trump used imagery with the subtlety of a train wreck during his campaigns. "Mexico is not sending us their best. They're bringing drugs. They're bringing crime. They're rapists." As racist, xenophobic, and vile as that statement was, it depicted an image that resonated with his base and helped Trump win the election. Democrats don't have to pander to the worst in human sentiment to win the hearts and votes of Americans, but they do need to paint an image that resonates with voters.

In chapter 3, we explore techniques for using positive emotions to promote the Democratic brand.

Define the Brand

A Reuters/Ipsos early exit poll in 2016 found that 68 percent believed "traditional parties and politicians don't care about people like me."*

Millions allowed Ronald Reagan's words from his first inaugural address to seep into their worldview of politics: "Government is not the solution to our problem; government

---

* Chris Kahn, "U.S. Voters Want Leader to End Advantage of Rich and Powerful: Reuters/Ipsos Poll," Reuters, November 8, 2016, https://www.reuters.com/article/us-usa-election-poll-mood/u-s-voters-want-leader-to-end-advantage-of-rich-and-powerful-reuters-ipsos-poll-idUSKBN1332NC.

is the problem."

Democrats don't believe that. We believe in a strong, smart, responsive government that works for every citizen's "pursuit of happiness."

If you look back at the issues Democrats own—caring for the sick, the elderly, the poor; caring about women's and minorities' rights; caring about the environment; protecting citizens from lax gun laws and greedy corporations—we see a theme emerge: *Democrats care about people*. We don't prioritize the rights of the superrich, corporations, or lobbyists. We prioritize the rights and lives of everyday Americans.

We are of the people; we are for the people. Heck, it's in our name: *Democratic* is derived from *dêmos*, meaning "common people."

We are proudly the party of the common people.

The Democratic brand must be consistent in order to permeate the consciousness of the millions who rarely, if ever, watch news shows or read newspapers. With all that in mind, we propose that our team, Democrats everywhere, make this our brand:

"Democrats Fight for the People."

When a voter goes into the voting booth and sees a list of candidates for local offices about whom he or she knows little or nothing, a snap decision is about to be made. Right now, there likely is no Democrat brand stuck in his or her head.

Let's change that.

A year from now, or ten years from now, voters should think, "Oh yeah, Democrats care about people." They should think that because we *do* care about people.

People first.

Define the Opposition

It's not just about saying what you're for; you also have to show what you stand against. A strong brand resolves a tension. It has a clearly defined "enemy" it goes up against. Nothing rallies people together behind a cause better than a clear opponent on the other side.

As mentioned above, Republicans use strong negative branding on Democrats, and we have to fight back by defining *them*. In our case, we must show that Republicans care almost exclusively about corporations and the rich. This is the flip side of our brand.

They are the party of big money, and we are the party *of the people*.

Those of us who follow politics know that about the parties, but most voters have no idea that's the case.

Ever since Trump took over the GOP and continues to have his party in a death grip, we can say with conviction that:

Republicans are anti-science, anti-facts, anti-expertise.

Democrats trust science, truth, and competence.

Remind voters that during the worst of the COVID-19 pandemic Trump and his acolytes continually mocked high-level scientists, and in the months since he left office that trend became worse. Republican governors blocked desperately needed commonsense mask mandates in schools, putting millions of students and staff at risk.

Republicans are the party of small issues—dictating who goes to which bathroom, blocking critical race theory, deriding sincere kneeling in protest, etc.

Democrats are the party of the big issues—**clean air, soil, and water; health care for all; a fair tax code; quality education for all; good paying jobs**; etc.

These defining party characteristics give us clarity in what we fight for and something real to fight against.

We must build our brand while simultaneously negatively branding the Republicans.

Define Yourself: Don't Let Others Define You

Liberal used to mean willing to consider a wide variety of views. Then the Right claimed the word stands for all kinds of nefarious things: open borders, freedom for criminals, illicit drug use, and so on.

So we became progressives. That has a nice ring to it, but

now it, too, has been commandeered by the Right to mean something bad.

When asked or confronted by the word *progressive*, or merely *Democrat*, always be ready to explain, in clear language, what that word means to you.

As in,

> "Yes, I am proudly a strong Democrat, but not by your Fox News scare-tactic definition. I stand for clean air and water, fair housing, better education for our kids, and a tax policy that makes sure those who have reaped the greatest gains from our American system pay their fair share. I want everyone to be able to get good quality health care without worrying about going bankrupt. I want all people, regardless of race, religion, or sexual orientation to have the same shot at success as everyone else. Which of those goals do you have a problem with?"

Seriously, do that. It's fun.

Slogans

"I'm with Her." You remember that slogan from Hillary Clinton's presidential campaign. While the story goes that it was written by a member of the "design team," presumably consultants agreed to make that slogan an integral part of the branding of Secretary Clinton.

But it was a weak slogan.

Slogans are something of a hybrid—part branding, part marketing. They are meant to apply to a specific candidate and last throughout the one specific campaign. Slogans rarely live to be a part of a reelection campaign.

Above all, a strong slogan should help push the undecided voters toward your candidate. But "I'm with Her" resonates only for those who already mentally hopped on the Clinton bandwagon. How did it move others to come aboard? It didn't.

What vision of the future did it offer? None.

What did it say about what she stood for and believed in? Nothing.

How did it suggest she will make *my* life better? Who knows?

During the 2016 presidential campaign, it did none of those things. It was generic, something that any female candidate could use. (And we should point out that "I'm with Him" would be equally insipid.)

A great slogan should quickly, simply, and powerfully communicate a core aspect of what the candidate believes in. It should be memorable and resonate deeply with what voters are looking for. It should connect to what Democrats believe in overall so that it helps build the Democrat brand. It should give people a rallying cry that gets them behind you.

And one more thing: a great slogan is about the voter, not the candidate.

"Make America Great Again" did all the above. It's simple. It has a vision of the future, even if that vision is going back to a nonexistent past. For conservative voters, it's emotional, and it resonates with their values and the values they associate with the Republican Party.

As usual, Democrats had no response. They had no clear idea of their own to fight back against this powerful branding message. "I'm with Her" was a classic limp slogan.

The then-senator Barack Obama had a powerful message and campaign with the slogan "Change We Can Believe In." He was the change candidate, and he came along when the country was hungry for a change. That slogan showed his vision and what he stood for in a way that resonated with what the country was feeling. The chant "Yes we can!" further emphasized that this change was possible, and it served as a rallying cry to bring people together around the idea. It helped build a movement around it. Unfortunately, that momentum was short lived, as Democrats strayed from these messages and didn't have anything to follow it with.

Great advertising agencies come up with great taglines all the time. Democrats should use them to help write and test different articulations of what we believe in and stand for.

The talent is there. Let's use them.

Words Matter—Words *Really* Matter

Blue Diamond sells almonds. Tons of almonds. But they might sell a whole lot less if they were not so careful about the words on their packages. One of their bags of nuts, for instance, tells us it contains "Oven-Roasted Almonds."

Would they sell less if it simply said, "Roasted Almonds"? Probably.

Wait. Aren't all roasted almonds cooked in an oven? But it's apparent Blue Diamond's marketing research showed that for some reason we salivate more over "oven-roasted" foods than just plain old "roasted" ones.

Then again, how many bags would they sell if the product merely offered "cooked" almonds? You also may have noticed that some foods are now made with "Fire-Roasted Tomatoes."

Hmm. Again, once you put something in an oven, fire is likely the heat source! But marketers have discovered that "fire roasted" sounds way better than "roasted" or merely "cooked" tomatoes.

Financial marketers discovered that when offered a choice between a "Lifetime annuity" or a product promising a "Guaranteed Income for Life," consumers preferred the latter, even though they're the same product.

Most of you reading this book will recall that polls showed early on that a majority of Americans disapproved of Obamacare but gave a thumbs-up to the Affordable Care Act. Yes, they are one and the same.

Republican strategist Frank Luntz wrote an entire book on this topic, *Words That Work. It's Not What You Say, It's What People Hear*. He is credited with turning the estate tax into the "death tax." Oil drilling became "energy exploration." He knew renaming these and many other phrases could sway public opinion simply by choosing the right words. Republicans take this seriously; we must as well. That is why no campaign can be blasé about words, especially those words meant to encapsulate an issue—antichoice, gun safety, voter suppression, etc.

The difference between "oven roasted" and "roasted" appears minimal to most of us, but branding honchos take nothing for granted. Nor should anyone involved in political campaigns.

One carefully chosen word can sway an election.

"Make America Great" is a put-down; "Make America Great Again" helped put Trump in the White House.

Again was one—massively effective—word.

Be Wary of Focus Groups

Focus groups have been a staple of political messaging for decades. But Democrats use them in the wrong way.

We should not be *following* the polls and focus groups; we should be *leading* them.

We follow focus groups when we blindly use messaging that "tests well." Often voters will say they like ideas and messaging that best match with what they already know. They tend to fear and reject new ideas that haven't already been understood and accepted. A classic example: before the *Seinfeld* TV show was released, it tested terribly in focus groups, apparently because it was too different from what people were used to.

If we haven't clearly established the ideas we want people to believe, then they won't test well. We must lead them there.

We must boldly state our convictions and repeat them until we hear them played back to us in focus groups.

When used well, focus groups can provide valuable information on what voters are thinking and how well your messages are landing with them. But there are many drawbacks. People tell you what they think you want to hear. They will be affected by social pressures and groupthink. They can be swayed, consciously or unconsciously, by the agenda, by the framing of the questions, and by the moderator. (Daryl Weber has substantial experience designing and leading focus groups.)

Worst of all, they often don't know their own true

motivations or intentions, because these are more emotional and subconscious than we realize. Instead, they will try to find rational justifications for their actions, which are often incomplete or misleading.

So we can't trust focus groups to guide us. We should tell the story and messages we know are right and true; then we can use focus groups to ensure those messages are being heard and understood the way we intend.

We can test *how* we say something, but not *what* we should be saying.

Frank Luntz has used focus groups effectively in this way for Republicans for decades. He knows the ideas he wants to get across, and then uses research to understand how people receive them. He also tests different words and languages to communicate those messages.

As he says, "It's not what you say; it's what people hear."

Be Wary of Consultants

For some reason, Democrats keep hiring the same political consultants, year after year, whether they win or lose. These consultants tend to use the same playbook for every election cycle regardless of the outcome.

This is the playbook that has kept Democrats from winning strong majorities in local and national elections for decades, despite overwhelming support for their policy positions. Presumably Hillary Clinton had top-notch consultants working diligently for her quest to become president. Yet they made blunder after blunder. Why, for just one glaring example, did she never set foot in Wisconsin? That alone was astonishing malpractice. What branding message did that send to the voters of that critical swing state?

Why do we, Democrats at every level, keep doing the same thing if it's only marginally working? Or not working?

Some of the past strategies have been great for the consultants, but not so great for Democrats or the American people. Consultants, we have to recognize, often have a built-in conflict of interest. While they have a broad range of options to recommend, some might want more television ads, which *might* be what's needed, or they might be getting a cut of the ad placements.

Conversely, they may earn less by recommending the branding techniques we talk about in this book, many of which earn them nothing above their set fees. All we're saying here is—please be wary and don't follow consultants blindly.

Regardless, it's time we brought in fresh thinking. Republicans often come from business backgrounds and tend to have a better, more intuitive sense for marketing and branding. To counter that, Democrats should start making better use of advertising, design, digital, and other agencies that are the top-tier experts in branding, communication, and selling. Plenty of folks in those worlds are staunch Democrats. We need to find them and take advantage of their experience and expertise to help build the Democratic brand.

While there are differences between selling toothpaste and candidates, both are about persuasion. The fundamentals are the same: you create powerful messages that resonate with people emotionally, tell those messages well, and repeat them often.

Remember, our suggestion here is about building the overall Democratic brand. It's an exercise in brand building more than vote counting (at first), so let's turn to expert brand builders. Political consultants have their place, but they are different from people who have true experience and competence in building and maintaining brand loyalty.

Let's find them, nurture them, and use them.

The same old consultants will get the same old results. We can't afford that.

Chapter 2 Summary

- Build the Democratic brand: "**Democrats Fight *for the People*.**"
- Define your opposition; Republicans only care about corporations and the rich.
- Define yourself; don't let others define you.
- Branding must feel personal to the voter.
- Be wary of focus groups.
- Be wary of consultants.
- Develop slogans that demonstrate our beliefs and rally voters behind our cause.
- No party is out to intentionally destroy the country. But considerable differences exist in their understandings of how to *improve* the country. Republicans believe you do so by helping *big money* and *big business* succeed. Democrats believe you do this by helping *people* succeed. It's the bottom-up approach, and it's much more effective.
- "**Fighting for the People**" is a memorable, clear, and sufficiently emotional foundation upon which to build a successful brand identity, but only if we sell it consistently and defend it convincingly.

SELLING THE DEMOCRATIC BRAND

Stay on brand. Stay on brand. Stay on brand.

All political advertising must stay on brand.

It's infuriating to see a political TV ad with no indication that the candidate is a Democrat. This goes back to "Democrats make each candidate start from zero." It's counterproductive. Stay on brand, and stay on the bigger message: **"Democrats Fight *for the People*."**

Every ad that strays from the brand dilutes the message from that particular candidate. It does nothing to help other Democrats; it diffuses the brand. It's lose-lose. Why do we keep doing that?

Our messages must be concise and consistent with the

Democratic brand. Attention spans are limited.

A Modest Proposal: Branding Videos

According to the nonpartisan Center for Responsive Politics (now recognized as OpenSecrets), during the 2020 election campaign, Americans spent an astonishing $14 billion on their preferred candidates, smashing previous records.[*]

Worse, aside from the immorality of that much money being spent for political purposes, Democrats nearly doubled the spending by Republican candidates. In spite of that flood of money in their favor, Democrats narrowly won the White House and did worse than expected in congressional elections.

This is a sorry state of affairs.

So it's time to try something drastically new:

Take a large chunk of campaign money and use it to produce and air high-quality Democratic *branding* commercials. And then air those ads on television and across all media—for a long time.

These TV and social media ads would highlight Democratic

---

[*] OpenSecrets.org, "2020 Election to Cost $14 Billion, Blowing Away Spending Records," OpenSecrets News, October 28, 2020, https://www.opensecrets.org/news/2020/10/cost-of-2020-election-14billion-update/.

values. **No candidate would be named.** The sole purpose would be to remind voters, and especially newer and younger voters, which team always fights for *them*.

This strategy helps every candidate in every election up and down the ballot. It would include several well-produced thirty- or sixty-second videos, featuring a variety of Americans, each speaking directly to the camera, explaining—ideally on location and in their own words—why they vote for Democrats.

Visualize a:

Doctor: "I'm a Democrat because we need good affordable health care for all Americans."

Student: "I support Democrats because we should all be able to get a great education without being burdened by debt for most of our lives."

Senior: "Democrats invented Medicare and Social Security. They will always protect those programs."

Young woman: "I never want to have an abortion. But if I come to that difficult decision, that's for me to decide, not you, and that's why I support organizations like Planned Parenthood and the Democratic Party that fights for them."

Teacher: "Democrats understand the importance and value of a good education for every student from pre-K through college."

Construction worker: "My union supported me throughout my whole life, and Democrats supported working men and women in the past and will in the future."

Scientist: "As a scientist and researcher, I know there is no substitute for factual, verifiable information. That's why I'm a Democrat."

Soldier: "One party waves the American flag and uses cheap slogans; the other party actually gives real help during and *after* military service. Yes, I'm a Democrat."

Priest: "The Bible taught us to be humble and aid those in need. I believe that, and so do my fellow Democrats."

Gay couple: "We don't want or need the government telling us who we can love. We always support Democrats."

And so on.

Imagine if this type of ad played frequently on all TV channels and across social media. We might finally reach the voters who "think" they are apolitical, but who in fact do have political issues that touch their lives. We might finally begin to shift that small slice in the middle—that 1 percent who can move so many elections over to us, now and well into the future.

It might seem risky to try something new. But staying on the current path will only continue to fail us.

A Modest Proposal II: Branding Templates

Every two years Democrats spend vast sums on 435 campaigns for the House of Representatives. Each campaign hires its own consultants and ad firms to craft a localized message for the candidates. The ads they develop tell us things we may or may not know about the candidate—no matter what is said, though, the other side will proclaim she or he is a socialist. Or crooked. Or voted for bad things.

It will likely be far smarter and certainly more efficient to stop doing all that. Let's break the mold.

Instead, let's put big bucks and resources behind developing a branding template for all Democratic candidates, a template that reminds voters of where the party stands on crucial issues.

The women in Iowa cities share the same concerns about their bodies as the women on Long Island. The college students in Northern California worry about student debt and climate change just like their pals in suburban Texas. The father of three anywhere in America stays up at night thinking about health care costs. And so on.

The DNC, or whatever the relevant group might be, would hire the best, most creative people to develop TV spots, radio ads, print and social media ads, and those would be shared by our candidates everywhere.

This one step has the potential to lift the quality and impact of Democratic campaign efforts. And the effect would be immediate.

Obviously, the campaigns can be augmented for local issues. But the *branding* message of Democrats does not and should not vary from district to district nor from state to state.

If all of us Democrats stand proudly with our party on the issues that affect the most people—the issues that help ensure a bright, safe, and prosperous future for our country—then that should be enough! Those are the nationwide issues that we need to instill into the consciousness of the voters, and we ought to do it in every campaign, through every election cycle, in every district across America.

A Modest Proposal III: Sell the Good News

Joe Biden took the presidential oath amid a deadly pandemic and a severe economic calamity. He, along with the Democratic Party, pushed for and passed the American Rescue Plan. By any measure, it was a resounding success.

But as months pass, victories fade from the headlines, and what happened to Obama and the Democrats in 2010 could happen again in coming elections. Good news is too often quickly forgotten.

Democrats need to remind voters what they accomplished for America. The Biden White House developed a terrific website (whitehouse.gov/american-rescue-plan/) that beautifully summarizes, as the site notes, "PRESIDENT BIDEN'S

PLAN TO PROVIDE DIRECT RELIEF TO AMERI-CANS, CONTAIN COVID-19, AND RESCUE THE ECONOMY."* And it gets its message across with smart text and appealing graphics.

Too bad the site will be unseen by 99.9 percent of voters.

That is why Democrats should pump out TV and social media campaigns to *continually* remind voters of Biden's—and the Democratic Party's—successes.

Waiting until we are deep in the election campaign season is too late! Branding doesn't happen according to a calendar. It happens—or it should happen—throughout the year, every year.

Find the good news—the news that makes lives better—and *sell it!*

Year-round positive-image-building branding will be considerably more cost-effective than the biannual deluge of dollars that takes place as election day approaches.

Branding. It's all about long-term branding.

---

* "The American Rescue Plan," The White House (The United States Government, October 8, 2021), https://www.whitehouse.gov/american-rescue-plan/.

A Modest Proposal IV:
Stop Most Politician-Specific Advertising

Seriously.

This is our most radical proposal, but likely the most impactful: No more ads telling the public how wonderful our candidate is and how dreadful the opponent is.

> **We suggest Democrats channel those billions of dollars we now spend on *politician-specific* advertising into *branding* campaigns to boost awareness of Democratic values.**

It seems beyond question that the one-shot ads bashing Republican opponents clearly have limited effect, and they turn voters, especially young voters, against the whole election process.

If it's true that most voters are not heavy consumers of reliable news providers—and it is—then the biannual blizzard of political ads quickly becomes meaningless static. Nothing stands out—nothing makes sense to voters as each side screams, "I am great! She is terrible!" Voters, busy with their own lives, cannot adjudicate the conflicting nonstop messages.

But a true branding campaign sidesteps all that brain-numbing noise. It implants feelings. It educates voters about our most important party-wide issues.

Unlike the original "Modest Proposal" satire published by Jonathan Swift in Britain in 1729, our proposals, asking for a significant reset of traditional Democratic marketing strategies, are definitely not satire. These proposals could very well swing more elections over to the blue team. Yes, they require a new mindset; we hope they are looked at with careful consideration.

All Democrats want voters to mark their ballots for our team from top to bottom. Branding, more than advertising, can help achieve that goal.

As for specific campaigns, they can, if they so choose, piggyback on to the branding ads, perhaps along the lines of, "*Like all Democrats, I believe in . . .*"

Since we grudgingly accept that our modest proposals won't gain traction immediately, we will continue to offer advertising suggestions in these pages.

Use Testimonials

It's nice when the voice-over artist in a well-produced TV or social media ad says something good about a candidate. It's way better when an actual citizen tells us why that candidate is splendid. And it's better still when someone of prominence—a retired military leader, a scientist, a beloved actor—assures us, *in their own words*, that the candidate deserves our vote.

Hillary Clinton might have become our president had she

used this most basic marketing tool. Too many people saw her as cold, calculating, and untrustworthy. Yet there are hundreds of people who know her, who worked with her, who interacted with her on many levels, who could have counteracted the negatives and boosted her positives.

Testimonials from community members or from political colleagues—or best of all, when possible, from Republicans—carry much more oomph than any other "I'm great; he's terrible" traditional marketing.

It's amazing that more Democratic candidates—the candidates who, after all, are fighting *for* the people—don't use testimonials *from* the people to garner maximum bang for the advertising buck.

Tap Into Emotions

In the marketing and branding world, the accepted wisdom is: people make decisions based on emotions and use logic for confirmation.

Republicans understand this better than Democrats. Emotions sell cars, watches, and Doritos. Emotions, far more than logic, also sell candidates.

When Trump wanted to make immigration an issue, he rarely talked about the broad numbers—with any truth, anyway—or the array of complicated concerns surrounding immigration. Instead, he would graphically describe one particular instance of a brutal rape or murder, allegedly committed by an undocumented immigrant, and how the victim's family is now grieving. When he spoke about China—and most voters have little or no expertise regarding international trade policy—he made a simplified "us versus them" argument that appealed to our patriotism.

Democrats need to learn that lesson.

In the health care debate, for example, we should explain it on the most personal level. One suggestion: use actual names. *Real people with genuine names are far more powerful than general themes.*

We can relate, for example, to Kate and Mike Richardson.

Kate is an army veteran who worked at the Walmart in Santa Fe. Mike did two tours in Iraq and then became an EMT. They have three kids—two young girls and a sixteen-year-old boy. But Kate was laid off during the pandemic, and Mike got knocked down with a severe case of COVID-19, which kept him from work for three months. Worse, they both lost their health insurance.

What do Republicans say to Kate and Mike Richardson? Basically, they say, "Sorry, you're on your own." But Democrats have been pushing for years to build a better health care system, one that protects patriotic, hardworking families like the Richardsons.

To be clear, that is a hypothetical but realistic scenario. There are hundreds of thousands of actual families like this. Find them, ask permission, and then tell their stories.

Again, on the flip side, Trump made immigration an issue by talking about one illegal immigrant who, he claimed, murdered a couple of people. He used specifics, and that story frightened people.

Whenever possible, bring every issue down to its most granular, most personal, most relatable story. Tap into the emotions that every voter harbors inside.

Statistics bore voters; evocative stories hold attention.

Use emotional hooks whenever you can. *Fear. Greed. Love. Loss. Patriotism.* And yes, even *tribalism*, if appropriate.

Use them judiciously, but use them. Don't let Republicans own those emotions.

Stay Positive

An old saying in marketing posits that "Half of your marketing budget is wasted, but you'll never know which half."

Well, maybe that is not always the case. It seems likely that a major marketing error made by Democrats has been an overreliance on negative ads. Democrats like to say—or our consultants make ads that say—"Our opponents are horrible, terrible, nasty people." And sure, they do the same to us.

While the jury is still out on the effectiveness of negative advertising in turning out voters, we can extrapolate advice from what the biggest marketers in the country do when it comes to television ads for prescription drugs.

Every disease or malady is obviously sad and negative. The advertisers could darkly warn about the bad things that will befall you by not taking their meds. Instead, their ads—*all* their ads—are buoyant and brightly positive. At the end of the commercial, every person is smiling!

Those massively expensive ad campaigns send a clear message, one based on their never-ending market research, and that message always boils down to *take our medicine and feel good!*

Projecting a positive, feel-good message about your product or service is basic branding. That's why you have never seen Coke bash Pepsi. Rolex never disses Breitling. BMW, Audi, and Lexus all stay in their lane by branding themselves as luxury experiences, and they do that without knocking the competition.

We should learn from and take advantage of that massive market research. It's likely we can gain voters by shifting from dark, negative marketing to more positive branding messages that trigger feel-good endorphins.

Vote for Democrats and feel great about yourself and your country.

America *is* a great country with a bright future. And our

candidates are the best equipped to take us into that bright future. Let's get *that* message out there.

Negative ads will always be a part of the landscape, especially as the GOP sinks deeper into its weird alternate reality. But our core values seek a bright future for all of us, and we should share that vision via our branding, wherever possible.

Ronald Reagan created a masterful positive message with his vision of a "shining city on a hill" and "morning in America." This was emotional, forward-looking, and optimistic. It gave people a clear, tangible picture of the future he would create for them. In its own way, Trump's "Make America Great Again" did this as well.

Democrats now need to show *our* positive vision of the future. It's an America where everyone, no matter who they are, has an equal and fair shot. Where we have a clean planet, accessible health care, quality education, and so much more. In essence, we're making a world where everyone can thrive.

People want to feel happy and secure. We can do that for them.

Let's tell them that. Positively.

Build the Base

We're talking here of the underlying base of Democrats in office everywhere. The president is the top of the pyramid, and below him or her are the thousands of officeholders in every locale.

It's a fact: state and local elections are the bedrock of political power in America. We need those people. Our party cannot thrive without a strong, enthusiastic, and widespread base of officeholders who bubble up through the ranks.

(A plug here for the organization Run for Something. From their site: "Run for Something is a grassroots-powered organization that recruits and empowers young progressives running for local office, with the goal of winning permanent power for decades to come."[*] In an email to supporters in early March 2021, they wrote, "Since Election Day 2020, over 12,000 young progressives have signed up to Run for Something!" That's fantastic. Check them out at runforsomething.net)

Plus, we need those folks to help fight gerrymandering, voter-suppression bills, and all the other issues that are dealt with by town, city, county, and state governments. And that again is why we need all Democrats to help build the Democratic brand.

Without positive branding, most of these folks face the daunting task of campaigning in a vacuum. It's nonsensical to make them do that. Sure, they will have their local party teams

---

[*] "Run for Something," Run For Something, November 19, 2021, https://runforsomething.net/.

to help, but strong national branding will greatly increase their chances.

In marketing and branding, everything matters. Take, for example, something as apparently simple as . . .

Yard Signs

Yes, yard signs. And buttons and T-shirts. It happens before every election. Yard signs pop up like wildflowers. And just about every sign contains a generic message, a message that can be said by any candidate anywhere at any time:

Joe Smith for City Council
Experience Counts

You can see them in yards, on the sides of streets, in store windows, and many do not indicate party affiliation. Why? *Are they embarrassed that they belong to a great party?*

It's likely we can improve the chances of the political base by using those signs to build the brand. What reason is there for Joe Smith and every one of our candidates to hide their loyalties? When voters look at the ballot, they see that Joe Smith is a Democrat, so what's the point of being coy on the yard signs?

Not one voter will choose a candidate because of a generic

yard sign. So rather than placing bland, generic messages on these ubiquitous signs, we suggest all our candidates include on their signs:

PROUD AMERICAN
PROUD DEMOCRAT

Those four words tie Democrats to patriotism, and they say that the candidate is part of a movement, that he or she cares about that movement, and that maybe the undecided voter might want to know about that movement.

The words "PROUD AMERICAN, PROUD DEMO-CRAT," seen on thousands of signs, plus bumper stickers, buttons and balloons, T-shirts, and in ads, over many years, can boost the image of our party.

Together these create a grassroots movement. They show we're not running from the labels Republicans and conservative media give us. Rather, we're proudly owning it as a badge. These small reminders, repeated consistently, proudly, and frequently, help build the perception of a proud Democratic movement, one that you want to join.

Let's do that.

Do Town Halls
Do More Town Halls

Meet your constituents in person. Assuming you can hold your own at these meetings, they will love you for it—usually.

Come prepared. Bring notes for expected topics. Have them laid out on your lectern, where you can see them easily, and don't be afraid to use them. You want to be accurate.

Use visual aids when you can. We live in a society that revolves around memes and visual media. We need to recognize and exploit that fact.

For instance, imagine Joe Biden holding up a photo of Trump with Lavrov and Kislyak while talking about how Trump, postpresidency, can't be trusted with our national security. That would be vastly more effective than merely talking about it.

But please ensure that your visual aids look professional. At the very least, have a graphic designer work their magic on your graphics. A top-flight professional is best, obviously, but for a onetime use you can get great low-cost results by using the freelance websites out there, like Fiverr.com or Upwork.com.

Even better, the Democratic National Committee (DNC) could and should create an asset library of visual aids that can be used by all Democrats. Logos, icons, charts, etc. Again, why have everyone reinvent the wheel?

Remain friendly—as long as you can! Be honest and direct.

When you don't know something, say so, but promise to get back to that person with an answer. And be sure to follow through on that promise.

Bring staff with you and use them when you are stumped. It's better to be seen as someone who seeks accuracy rather than someone who bluffs their way through tough questions. Let the other side be the party of made-up "facts."

And if you can, if the opportunity arises, do what Wisconsin's Representative Mark Pocan and others have done: town halls in a neighboring district! When then-Speaker of the House Paul Ryan refused to appear in front of his constituents while advocating for controversial issues, Pocan went to several parts of Ryan's district to do the town halls Ryan should have.

Stop Being a Punching Bag

They play dirty. We don't.

Individually, all politicians say things that are less than fully accurate. Republicans, however, have no reservations about severely bending or totally ignoring the truth. (This began with Rush Limbaugh and was perfected by Trump.) And their dark-money PACs are even worse. Some of them have published deeply offensive ads—prime examples include those pushed out against Jon Ossoff during his congressional campaign that came close to being overtly anti-Semitic.

We should *never* sink to their level, but we don't have to be saints. Saints don't win elections.

We have to hit back *hard*. Hillary let Trump walk all over her in the debates. She could have forcefully countered everything he threw at her, but she chose to stay above the fight. The result was that his attacks stuck.

One of the few times she parried his attack that she was "a terrible senator" was when she countered with, "Well, I was reelected with sixty-eight percent of the vote, so I guess I wasn't that bad." *Boom*. She could have counterpunched that way constantly during the debates, but she didn't.

Were the consultants to blame? Maybe. But Democratic candidates need to show much more backbone in debates and during press conferences.

When they label virtually every Democrat a "socialist" or "radical" or "radical socialist," we need to respond. By not responding, we implicitly suggest that those labels are accurate. Without a forceful response, their mere repetition makes them more deeply ingrained and harder to change in the minds of voters.

Please, let's stop that acquiescence to their lies.

Stop Sounding Wimpy. Here's How.

We see it all the time. A Democratic politician stands before an array of microphones poised to make an important point.

The crowd is with him, ready to explode with passion, but he starts one of his key sentences with "To me . . ."

And then a moment later he throws in "I believe . . ."

Stop doing that.

Those are two all-to-common examples of wimpiness by Democrats.

"To me" is wimpy. It says, "Um, you may think differently about rioters rampaging through the hallowed halls of the Capitol, and I respect your right to have that opinion, yada, yada."

Same with, "I believe." *No.* We "believe" things that can't be proven beyond doubt. We may believe in a higher power. We believe in the goodness of America. We believe the New York Jets will win another Super Bowl someday.

In a moment, we will outline specific wimpy words and phrases Democrats need to avoid.

Biden Does It Right—Sometimes

During his first town hall after taking office, President Biden was asked by a young woman about forgiving federal student debt. She wanted, as had been pushed by some in the progressive wing, $50,000 of her debt to be wiped off the books.

She concluded by asking, "When will you make that happen?"

"I won't make that happen,"* Biden immediately replied. And then he explained his position.

His bluntness was a bit startling. So startling that the next morning at least two TV commentators mentioned the exchange in a very positive way. They weren't referring to the policy issue itself, but instead they spoke of how refreshing it was to see a politician give a clear, blunt answer to a provocative question.

How sad that a direct, nonevasive reply from a politician was, literally, newsworthy!

Use Clear, Declarative Sentences—Stay Assertive

Here's your primer in power talk.

Stop saying "I think . . ."

As in, "I think we need to spend the money to fix our crumbling roads and bridges."

No. Just say, "We absolutely need to spend the money to fix our crumbling roads and bridges."

Avoid saying, "I believe . . ."

---

* "Remarks by President Biden in a CNN Town Hall with Anderson Cooper," in CNN Presidential Town Hall with Joe Biden, transcript, Cable News Network, February 16, 2021.

As in, "I believe that approach is wrong."

No! Just say, "That approach is wrong."

Avoid "In my opinion . . ."

We don't need your opinion. We don't need to know how you "feel" or what you *think* or what you *believe*. We want our leaders to assert themselves, to tell us right from wrong.

So ditch:

- "I hope . . ."
- "I pray . . ."
- "I wish . . ."
- "In my estimation . . ."
- "To my way of thinking . . ."

"The fact of the matter." Who talks that way? Only politicians. Just get to the point. As in, "These investments in infrastructure will pay for themselves." If you are not giving us *facts*, why are you wasting our time?

"We are at an inflection point." Who says that? Most folks could not define "an inflection point," so why say that?

Take command of the facts, and take command of your sentences.

Ditch the Clichés

We're sick and tired of everyone being sick and tired. Enough is enough! Because at the end of the day, you can't keep kicking the can down the road. After all, someone has to pay the piper. It's time to stand up for what you believe in!

A cliché gets you nowhere. It frequently doesn't advance the conversation. It doesn't make you look smart, and what's worse, it can make you look and sound like every other politician.

With just a tiny bit of thought, you can rewrite any cliché. For example, at the simplest possible level, instead of "sick and tired" you can say you are "tired of hearing . . ." Even that minor edit helps keep you from sounding like everyone else.

So think outside the box. The American people deserve better. Remember, it's a marathon, not a sprint. The only poll that counts is the one on election day. And so, my fellow Americans, we'll keep you in our thoughts and prayers.

Know Your Facts

It's well known that "Republicans do better with the economy." Poll after poll shows that's what Americans believe. And Trump continually brayed that his economic success was unmatched in all of American history.

That's even what many Democratic politicians believed.

It's what anchors on CNN and MSNBC believed. They still believe it today.

Too bad it ain't true! And what's worse, far worse, is that too many Democrats accept the "accepted wisdom" about economic matters.

So let's look at the facts.

First, the **job market**. Here's a CNN website headline from January 22, 2021:

"Biden Inherits Worst Job Market of Any Modern President."*

Got that? Donald Trump handed Joe Biden the worst job market in memory. Few Democrats—and even fewer news anchors—realize that.

And who inherited the second worst job market? Yep, it was what Obama inherited from George W. Bush!

That means two consecutive Republican presidents gave their Democratic successors horrendous economies.

Why don't the voters know that? Yes, it's because Democrats

---

* Eli Rosenberg, "Jobless Claims Remained at Historic Highs Last Week, as Biden Inherits the Worst Job Market of Any Modern President," *Washington Post*, January 21, 2021, https://www.washingtonpost.com/business/2021/01/21/900000-filed-jobless-claims-last-week-historically-high-level-biden-inherits-worst-job-market-any-modern-president/.

failed to tell them. And don't let Republicans complain, "Well, if it were not for COVID-19 . . ." Nope. A leader has to lead through good and bad times. Trump screwed up royally, and the job market suffered more than it should have.

Now let's look at the **stock market**. Did you know during the Obama administration *the stock market nearly tripled, and the unemployment rate was cut in half*?

And did you know that Trump never came close to that level of economic success?

Why don't you know that? Why don't reporters know that?

Yet the myth of Republican mastery of the economy persists. Democrats have those facts on their side, but they don't use them, because they don't know them.

What about **GDP**?

Here's what the *Los Angeles Times* said on October 27, 2020:

> But even looking at the three years before COVID-19 made a mess of things, the U.S. economy under Trump performed about the same as it had during the last three years under President Obama . . .
> Consider: Under Obama from 2014 to 2016, real gross domestic product—the broadest measure of economic activity—grew at an average annual rate of 2.5%. In Trump's first three years, 2017 to 2019, real GDP

expanded by an annual average of 2.6%, according to the Bureau of Economic Analysis.*

That completely refutes Trump's brash claims of an economic "turnaround" that was vastly better than anything seen before.

Here's a chart from the *New York Times*, February 2, 2021. The headline of the article by David Leonhardt was:

Why Are Republican Presidents So Bad for the Economy?: GDP, jobs, and other indicators have all risen faster under Democrats for nearly the past century.†

And take a look at who's down at the bottom of the list of modern presidents.

---

* Don Lee, "Trump vs. Obama: Who Has the Better Record on the Economy?," *Los Angeles Times*, October 7, 2020, https://www.latimes.com/politics/story/2020-10-27/trump-vs-obama-who-really-did-better-on-the-economy.
† David Leonhardt, "Why Are Republican Presidents So Bad for the Economy?," *New York Times*, February 2, 2021, https://www.nytimes.com/2021/02/02/opinion/sunday/democrats-economy.html.

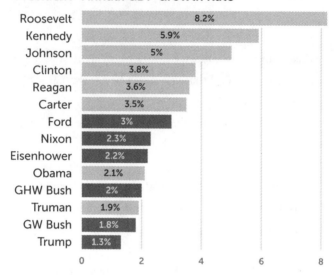

President | **Annual GDP Growth Rate**

Roosevelt — 8.2%
Kennedy — 5.9%
Johnson — 5%
Clinton — 3.8%
Reagan — 3.6%
Carter — 3.5%
Ford — 3%
Nixon — 2.3%
Eisenhower — 2.2%
Obama — 2.1%
GHW Bush — 2%
Truman — 1.9%
GW Bush — 1.8%
Trump — 1.3%

So, as these charts and stats make clear, **Republicans screw things up, and Democrats have to come in and clean up the mess.** Again and again.

Finally, consider **the national debt**—always a favorite target of Republicans.

Under Trump, despite his campaign promises to dramatically reduce the debt, the national debt *increased* by an additional trillion dollars—and that was *before* anyone heard about COVID-19.

Yet again, Democrats failed to use these powerful facts to tarnish the Republican brand. So let's turn around the false perception about which party is best for the economy. We do that first by learning and understanding the facts and then hammering people with those facts.

The headline question above, "*Why Are Republican Presidents So Bad for the Economy?*" is shiny political gold. It should be a frequent Democratic talking point. It's salient, it's powerful, and most importantly, it's true.

And the answer to that question, by the way, is that Republican presidents increase spending while giving tax breaks to the rich and powerful. As a result, the deficit explodes, and then Democrats come in and have to clean up the mess.

Democrats must be branded as the *Party That Boosts the Economy.*

There should be whole campaigns that pound that message: **Democrats Are Always Better for the Economy**.

Republicans *brag* about the economy, when they are in power. Democrats actually *improve* the economy. See the difference?

Use viewer-friendly statistics and charts or testimonials from experts. There are many ways to get that message across, but we must act quickly.

Stop ceding "who's best for the economy" to Republicans. *It's a big fat lie, so fight back against that false perception.* We cannot be shy about this issue!

It is way past time for Democrats to change the political

branding about the economy. Whether it's the economy, health care, taxes, the environment, or any other important issue facing the electorate, it behooves every Democratic candidate or staffer to do their "market research" and to use it effectively.

How to Look Like a Typical Politician When Being Interviewed

Rule number one: when you are asked a question that calls for a yes or no answer, don't reply with a direct yes or no. To illustrate how a lack of directness hurts politicians, consider the following: The morning of January 28, 2021, Senator Elizabeth Warren appeared on CNBC's *Squawk on the Street*. She was asked to give her views on the crazed GameStop trading frenzy. She pontificated about "the little guy" and the inequities in the markets and related topics.

The next day on that show, coanchor David Faber and his cronies were still discussing GameStop. After a while they brought up the Warren interview from the previous morning.

Suddenly, Faber stopped and said, "Honestly, I don't know *what* she was saying. Was she for more regulation, less, or something different?"*

---

* "Episode 1/29/2021," in *Squawk on the Street*, CNBC, January 29, 2021.

Exactly! I (Ken) saw that Warren interview as it happened, and I shouted at the screen, *"Just answer the question!"*

Of course, Senator Warren is an intellectual powerhouse, and she knows her stuff about how money sloshes around. But here she obfuscated her reply, and twenty-four hours later that dance was remembered.

Don't be that guy. Or woman. Everyone hears when you are evading the question. If you take more than one short sentence to give a direct answer, you have failed. And you are immediately diminished.

A side note here about a strange and annoying phenomenon that has begun afflicting TV interviewers over the past few years: Many of them now ask two or even three questions at once. As in, "Senator, what are the roadblocks to getting this bill to the president's desk? And if you think it won't pass, what steps do you plan to take to ensure your party never faces this position again, and who among your colleagues will support you on this?"

This fosters confusion for the viewer and oftentimes the interviewee as well, as in the glare of the lights and camera they have to remember all that was asked.

Generally, the best strategy is to answer the first question first. That's the one the viewers likely remember. Then, if you recall the other questions, get to those.

If you're feeling nicely secure in your skin, you can say,

with a smile, "Well, you asked me three questions. Let's look at the first one."

Perhaps if enough politicians do this we can get TV and radio hosts to stop that exasperating habit.

How to *Not* Look Like a Typical Politician When Being Interviewed

Be honest. Be succinct.

Show you understand *why* the question does or does not affect my life.

And answer the damn question immediately!

If you are on television (or Zoom), look directly into the camera.

We'll acknowledge here that some politicians are, for various reasons, taught to avoid direct answers, which may be wise from a fact-checking perspective, but it is highly suspect as a campaign strategy.

Speak *to* us. Chuck Schumer has an annoying tendency to look down as he makes important points, even when he's speaking without notes. Why has he never been coached to stop doing that?

And smile. George W. Bush won voters over by being "a guy you can have a beer with." You'll win a few more votes as well by projecting friendliness, but only when appropriate.

Don't force it, but do try to smile when it feels right.

Authenticity and friendliness score points.

Your Political ABCs

In the sales community, there is the ABC rule: "Always Be Closing."

Let's make our own political ABC rule: "**Always Be Campaigning**."

Always.

Use every opportunity to slip in a branding word or phrase. Remind voters of the slogans that brand you and your party. *No one remembers the specifics.* So instead, consider yourself a quarterback: How does this play, this interview, move the ball forward? Try never to go more than two or three sentences without scoring a branding point.

Modesty Doesn't Pay

We New Yorkers know that before he entered politics Donald Trump put his name on everything possible. We also knew before most others that he failed at many things: businesses, marriages, parenting. Putting his name in glittering letters atop buildings helped make him a brand name. He glorified his successes and ignored—or denied—his failures. That strategy worked for him in New York real estate, and when he entered politics he surely did not forget that lesson.

When his administration sent out COVID-19 relief checks, his name was on every single check. During the height of the pandemic, Trump held daily "press briefings," which, of course, morphed into puff-piece campaign rallies.

He bragged about his perceived victories, despite facts and logic saying those victories were illusory. Truth never got in the way of his nonstop bragging. He bragged about literally everything. And in the end, Trump was rewarded with eleven million more votes in 2020 than he received in his first campaign.

Democrats don't do that. To be reasonable, neither do most Republicans not named Trump, though they continue to support him single-mindedly. But we should understand and appreciate the power of bravado.

It was reported that President Biden briefly thought about putting his name on the COVID-19 relief checks his administration sent out, but he decided against it. Apparently, it would slow the process, and he wanted the money in people's accounts ASAP. The night the bill passed, MSNBC's Rachel Maddow suggested, giddily, that she would love to see Biden's name on the checks, adorned with glitter!

Humility is adorable. But self-confidence builds trust and pulls in the votes.

Bragging the wrong way, we must acknowledge, can be a double-edged sword. The prime example is "Obamacare." The media and the GOP public stuck Obama's name on the Affordable Care Act. Within weeks, Republicans successfully made "Obamacare" a dirty word, despite the fact that polls showed a majority of voters very much liked what was actually in the act.

Obama and the Democrats should have aggressively begun calling it "Obama's Affordable Care Act." Most voters didn't know what was in Obamacare; they just knew they didn't like it! Democrats should have pushed its virtues at every opportunity, but they didn't. And that was one more cause of the shellacking of the 2010 election.

"Modesty doesn't pay," by the way, is not a new concept in American politics. In a February 16, 2021, *Wall Street Journal* book review of *George Washington: The Political Rise of America's Founding Father*, Barton Swaim writes, "Washington was a savvy packager of his own personal virtues. He knew that if you don't engage in a bit of personal self-aggrandizement, you lose."* He also says, "To put the point brutally, you can't win elections if you're unable or unwilling to tell people, or

---

* Barton Swaim, "'George Washington' Review: Our Founding Politician ," *Wall Street Journal*, February 15, 2021, https://www.wsj.com/articles/george-washington-review-our-founding-politician-11613430102.

somehow communicate to them, how great you are."*

Trump never missed an opportunity to brag, whether the reason for his smugness was true or not. He was a despicable president, but millions think he was fantastic. They believe that *because he told us every single day how fantastic he was.*

We must never lie, must never cross lines of reasonableness, but voters gravitate to people who exude confidence. Hence military veterans look for a moment to remind you of their background. Same with prosecutors, successful businesspeople, physicians, and so on.

There's an old joke, with many variations:

What's ten seconds?

That's the maximum time from when you meet someone to when they let you know they went to Harvard.

Don't do that. Wait a full minute.

Humility might help get you into heaven, but it won't get you into office. Find ways to "somehow communicate to them" that you are damn good at what you do, that you are passionate about the issues, that you understand their needs and aspirations.

In the Sunday, January 24, 2021, issue of the *New York Times*, Ezra Klein wrote a featured opinion piece:

---

* Ibid.

The only callout in the article was:

"You don't get re-elected for things voters don't know about.***

Exactly. Tell them.

Then tell them again.

And again. Why? Because . . .

It Takes Seven "Touches"

In direct marketing circles, the accepted wisdom is that you need to get a message to a potential customer *at least* seven times before the message sticks. While that obviously can't apply to all situations, it's a great goal for political candidates.

One signing ceremony or one mention at a town hall or one answer to a reporter's question will have zero sticking power. Every message of importance must be repeated, um, repeatedly.

Thankfully, Democrats now recognize that Obama and his team, back when they had their first victories, missed their opportunity to make the point:

---

* Ezra Klein, "Democrats, Here's How to Lose in 2022. And Deserve It.," *New York Times*, January 21, 2021, https://www.nytimes.com/2021/01/21/opinion/biden-inauguration-democrats.html.

Biden aides and top Democrats have vowed to avoid what he sees as the Obama administration's disastrous mistake of not touting its early wins, particularly the 2009 stimulus that was ridiculed by Republicans and, Democrats believe, never received sufficient recognition for its role in saving the economy.*

Indeed. That reticence to aggressively tell the public about the truly outstanding things they accomplished led directly to the "shellacking" of 2010.

Whatever you're proud of, say it clearly, without any hesitancy or ambiguity, and say it at every opportunity.

Find Your Strength and Sell It

Democrats shy away from anything that seems like bragging. Trump, however, taught us that humility counts for naught in politics. He bragged about everything he claimed to have done, and truth rarely made an appearance.

We won't ever emulate that style, but we do need to let the public see us in the best possible light. Here's an illustration

---

* Annie Linskey, Tyler Pager, and Jeff Stein, "Biden Wants to Sell the Stimulus. The White House Is Still Figuring out How.," *Washington Post*, March 10, 2021, https://www.washingtonpost.com/politics/biden-stimulus-sales-pitch/2021/03/09/71dad6d4-80f9-11eb-9ca6-54e187ee4939_story.html.

of what we did wrong in Hillary's presidential run.

In 2012 our family was given a tour of an American ambassador's official residence by the ambassador herself. She was completely, um, diplomatic and reserved. But as the afternoon came to a close, I (Ken) casually mentioned that, as a New Yorker, her boss, Secretary of State Clinton, had served as my senator, and we were fans of her. The ambassador immediately dropped all her diplomatic façade and became effusive in her praise of Hillary Clinton. The ambassador explained she had been in the diplomatic corps for almost thirty years and had never experienced a secretary of state with the empathy, vision, and commitment of Senator Clinton.

Similarly, prior to the final months of the 2016 campaign, I had seen a good number of quotes from Republicans who praised Hillary's work ethic and her deep knowledge of the issues.

Yet, when Hillary ran against Trump, there was not one commercial, *not one*, that extolled the human side of her.

This was a fatal flaw in her campaign.

What were the consultants thinking? Why did they make no attempt to fix the prevailing narrative of Hillary as "aggressive," "ambitious," and "coldhearted"? Or worse, "crooked"? Republican strategists make shit up. In this case, we had all the facts on our side and didn't use them.

The lessons from the Hillary loss must not be forgotten:

Every candidate has strengths and weaknesses. Defend the weaknesses and burnish the strengths.

Don't let Republicans narrate our story. *We* must narrate our own story.

Find Your Weakness and Defend It Directly

According to an August 2016 *New York Times* poll, an astounding 67 percent of registered voters said Hillary Clinton was "untrustworthy."* Yet, as noted, people who knew her personally raved about her intelligence, compassion, and ethics.

Why did her team do nothing, absolutely nothing, to counter her biggest liability?

Why did most of her ads tell us how terrible Trump is instead of telling us—in clear, emotionally charged ways—how great *she* is?

In fact, she could have used quotes from John McCain and other top Republicans, *including Trump*, about how smart she is and how hard she works. Why were none of them used?

Democratic candidates need to attack their opponent's biggest weakness *and* defend their own perceived weakness.

---

* Michael Barbaro, "Americans Don't Trust Her. But Why?," *New York Times*, August 16, 2016, https://www.nytimes.com/2016/08/16/podcasts/hillary-clinton-trust.html.

Don't let it fester. The longer it's out there, and the more it gets repeated, the more it seems like truth to voters. That's exactly what happened to Hillary Clinton, and it's why a majority of voters went into the voting booth believing she was untrustworthy.

She was a victim of negative branding. It happens all the time.

Here's a quote from the *Washington Post*, November 14, 2020:

> "My opponent only talked about three words: Defund the police," Democrat Cameron Webb said on a private call this week, *Politico* reported. He lost what Democrats hoped was a winnable race in Virginia.
>
> "I'm not sure that as a party we took that attack head on, and provided our counter narrative," Rep. Stephanie Murphy (D-Fla.) told *Politico* of "socialist" attacks resonating with Hispanic voters in Florida, costing Democrats two House seats. "It's not enough to say what you're not; you have to define what you are. And we have to define it in a way that doesn't scare the American people."*

---

* Amber Phillips, "All the Reasons Democrats Say They Did Poorly down Ballot," *Washington Post*, November 14, 2020, https://www.washingtonpost.com/politics/2020/11/14/all-reasons-democrats-say-they-did-poorly-down-ballot/.

Those two paragraphs encapsulate the persistent problems of Democrats' campaigns.

Democratic candidates let Republicans set false narratives—"defund the police," and "socialist" attacks—while failing to sell the public on their own strengths.

Stop doing that. Don't let *any* attack on you grow into a full-blown characterization of who you are. Act quickly and decisively to turn the narrative about who you really are.

Or Admit Your Weakness and Make It a Strength

Imagine if Joe Biden, in a debate, said, "I sometimes stutter. It's something I've had to deal with all my life. I'll never be a great orator. I'll never get a crowd all fired up. So forgive me when I stumble on a few words now and then. Instead, I've dedicated my life to you, the American people. I promise you the truth, even when the truth is difficult."

Humility can be more powerful than bombast.

Above all, when you identify a weakness, don't ignore it. That only makes things worse. Instead, acknowledge a weakness in a way that boosts your image. It takes imagination, but with teamwork and a bit of mental effort, a solution can always be found.

Critique Your Performance

Every time you appear in public you are a performer. Sorry if that offends, but it's true. Therefore, you must think like a performer.

Consider this: Every actor, no matter how illustrious, depends on directors for guidance and honest—often brutally honest—feedback. You, Madam or Mister Candidate, are no different. You simply cannot see yourself the way others see you.

That said, at the very least, all your public appearances should be recorded. Then you should find time to watch—or listen, if it's radio or a podcast—to yourself. Take notes! Do not assume you will remember what you need to fix. You won't.

Every one of us has flaws, and by watching yourself on video you can see things you never realized you have been doing.

Some of the most common unforced errors include:

- Saying certain phrases too often;
- Unconscious coughs or tics;
- Laughing or smiling at inappropriate moments (looking at you, Kamala);
- Looking down while speaking (Hello, Chuck Schumer); and
- Rambling replies to questions (too many to mention!).

Accept that watching yourself on video is agony for just about everyone! Get over it; it's a vitally important exercise.

Better than watching yourself, of course, is to have a dispassionate, experienced, and trusted person give you feedback on your public appearances.

The best path, however, is to have a professional director or coach on your team. They likely won't be full-time, but any pro who can provide an honest evaluation on what you've done, as well as tips for improvement, will be an invaluable asset.

Regardless of who offers you feedback, always be gracious. The process is awkward for the other person as well. Listen carefully, take notes of what they say, and then thank them. Don't try to explain or argue—doing that will reduce the likelihood of getting a good critique the next time.

Be aware that often "director's notes," which seem off base at first, will make more sense to you in a day or two, after the emotion of the moment dissipates.

And while every appearance is a performance, you must never be seen as prepackaged or "performing" (Hello, Ms. Clinton). Naturalness is a required and acquired trait. The best—and really the only—way to achieve naturalness is through solid preparation followed by plenty of flight time.

Learn from Trump

There's a reason a semiliterate, frequently bankrupted reality TV "star," who had to pay a $25 million fine for fraud (Trump University) and who had his "charitable foundation" shut down, received more votes than any other Republican in history. Actually, there are many reasons. We can be stubborn and refuse to recognize the factors that caused millions of voters to give him unwavering loyalty, or we can hold our noses and learn.

Here are some strategies we can appropriate from the "other guy."

Look as good as you can. Trump was frequently mocked for wearing ill-fitting suits on his corpulent body. Nonetheless, he was always seen in a full dark suit, tie, and white shirt. He was always coiffed, and he wore makeup to, among other things, cover the bags under his eyes.

Speak with confidence. Yes, he was ridiculously confident, but that trait is very much what voters want in their leaders. Strength sells, weakness or indecision turns voters away.

Highlight accomplishments. Trump never missed an opportunity to brag about his accomplishments, real or imaginary. As we have stressed, the majority of voters have little knowledge of most issues, so they need constant reinforcement of "what have you done for me lately?"

Raise the stakes. Show what's at stake if we lose, and make it real and immediate for people. That was easy for Trump:

Anything connected to Democrats was apocalyptic. "If Biden wins, your 401(k) will be wiped out!" We don't play those games, but we certainly can warn against, for example, the dire threats of climate change and how America will fall behind the rest of the world if we don't maintain and upgrade our infrastructure and education systems.

Promise good times. We have to admit: "Make America Great Again" was a powerful slogan, despite his never specifying what era he meant to evoke. But you know, Democrats have plenty to offer when it comes to a bright future: more racial harmony; more acceptance of all people; a strong economy based on smart investments in renewable energy, infrastructure, and education; cleaner air to breathe; cleaner water to drink; and on and on.

Keep it simple. Trump was a master at making any policy— no matter how complex—an easy to understand, simple idea that anyone, even those who pay no attention to politics or policies, can understand. We have to boil down complex policies into their essential, emotional elements and then communicate only that. Anything else just dilutes and confuses the message.

Democrats need to stop explaining policies like they are in a college classroom and start telling stories like they are in a bar.

Tell stories. Without a script, Trump could barely put a coherent sentence together, yet he was able to construct clear stories in the minds of his followers. Stories have a hero and a villain, so he made sure everything he was trying to get done had a clear villain—Hillary, Obama, Pelosi, the press, or just "liberals"—and, of course, he was always the hero saving us from doom.

Our candidates can do the same. Personalize campaign issues; make everything relatable to the average citizen.

As we've said so often, Donald Trump was and is a repulsive figure, but he did get elected to the highest office in the land.

So let's reject the bad and learn from what he did well.

Understand and Exploit Social Media

Here's what we know about social media. Whatever "rules" there are today about how to win in that space will change by the time you get to the period at the end of this paragraph. That doesn't mean that you don't give it your best shot.

You may not realize that the apparently random nature of how things pop up on TikTok, Instagram, Facebook, or any other platform is far from random. Humans by the thousands, along with ever-changing algorithms, constantly tweak the systems to increase engagement. You cannot be haphazard in your approach to social media; you—or more likely, your team—need to spend time and money aiming at moving targets.

This applies particularly to crisis management. For example,

Twitter gives you an instant opportunity to apologize or correct a gaffe. A quick and heartfelt apology on Twitter for a misstatement can go a long way with voters.

Some of our smartest Democratic politicians are now frequently live streaming to answer questions and inform constituents about the legislative process. That's a wise choice for reaching a voter base that increasingly gets its information that way.

Probably the best social media advice is to recognize that:

1. You absolutely need to master social media.
2. You need smart young people to help you.

It can be mysterious. How can a seventeen-year-old get hundreds of thousands or even millions of followers? They do. And there are many of them.

You need to master social media because clearly the overwhelming majority of young voters could not care less about what Lester Holt or David Muir say on the evening news. They definitely are not swayed by the insightful writings of Thomas Friedman or Paul Krugman. But the latest influencer on TikTok? Yeah, that's the conduit to their still malleable brains. And as mentioned, even kids in middle school are only one or two election cycles away from being able to vote. And the fourteen-year-olds can influence their older siblings. Or their parents!

Some of these influencers are very young, and some are not. But if you can understand and harness their secret powers, you're going to win votes.

Eliminate Typos and Grammatical Gaffes

Here's a small but important point.

Avoid embarrassment. Everyone makes mistakes. That's why no candidate or candidate's representative should ever send out *anything* without having a competent second (or third) set of eyes check it carefully.

Whether it's a polished position paper or a spur-of-the-moment tweet, accept that you can and will make yourself look silly if you go it alone.

Covfefe, anyone?

And, of course, that second opinion can also help ensure that you are saying what you meant to say clearly and efficiently.

Fire on All Cylinders

Representative Alexandria Ocasio-Cortez drew national attention in June 2018 when she, in the Democratic primary, unexpectedly knocked out Joe Crowley, a respected ten-term congressman. She gets it.

As she told the *New York Times* on November 11, 2020:

> These folks [Dems who lost] are pointing toward Republican messaging that they feel killed them, right? But why were you so vulnerable to that attack? If you're not door-knocking, if you're not on the Internet, if your main points of reliance are TV and mail, then you're not running a campaign on all cylinders. . . . Sure, you can point to the message, but they were also sitting ducks. They were sitting ducks.*

AOC, then and now, understands that each vote counts and that we need to fight hard for every single one. In every election.

Her opponent in the 2018 primary was complacent. AOC was not, and she pulled off a stunning upset.

And now, in office, she basically continues to campaign at every opportunity. She is constantly livestreaming to answer questions and inform constituents about the legislative process—a valuable tool for reaching a voter base that increasingly gets its information that way.

---

* Alexandra Ocasio Cortez, "Alexandria Ocasio-Cortez on Biden's Win, House Losses, and What's Next for the Left," interview by Astead W. Herndon, *New York Times*, November 7, 2020, https://www.nytimes.com/2020/11/07/us/politics/aoc-biden-progressives.html.

At this point, she seems to have a lock on her district, but she behaves as if she could lose her edge in the polls at any moment. This attitude not only helps her but *it helps other Democrats*.

And for the sake of completeness, please know that our advice is for *all* Democrats, regardless of where they fall on the political spectrum.

Which leads to our next point.

Support the Party
Support Other Democrats

It was weird and maddening.

In the 2016 election, some Democratic candidates—for Senate and elsewhere—wouldn't even say whether they had voted for Obama! They were coy about who they supported. *And they ended up losing anyway*. Why? It's likely because voters sensed there was no "center" to the candidates—no core values.

It was embarrassing to the party, and it resulted in a futile effort.

Will future Democratic candidates learn from that? Not if history is a guide. As Bill Maher angrily and correctly pointed out in his June 30, 2017, interview with Dan Savage, Republicans support each other. He mentioned how Jon Ossoff, in his run for a House seat, distanced himself from Nancy Pelosi and from much of the party.

Did that work? Of course not. *It never does.*

But when Ossoff ran for Senate in 2020, he changed. He became more assertive, and yes, far more identifiable as a true Democrat.

And he won. In Georgia!

His team branded him as a progressive Democrat with progressive ideas. He stood apart, clearly, from his opponent.

As a friend once remarked, "Coke will never sell more cans by positioning themselves as similar to Pepsi." In other words, if you are proud of your progressive ideas, say so! Be proud of your brand.

Perhaps the thinking in our party is slowly changing. We hope so. But we know our party is widely diverse, and many forces can cause our candidates to backslide.

Stay vigilant.

Chapter 3 Summary

- Stay on brand!
- Consider making branding videos that build the Democratic brand overall.
- Start saying you are a "proud Democrat" everywhere you can.
- Use testimonials.
- Tap into emotions.
- Help build the entire Democratic base of candidates.
- Use yard signs to build the brand.
- Do town halls. Do more town halls.
- Stop being a punching bag.
- Learn how to stop sounding wimpy. Use clear, declarative sentences, and ditch the clichés.
- Know your facts! The truth is on your side!
- Don't look like a typical politician.
- Remember your ABCs: **Always Be Campaigning.**
- Bang your own drum. Modesty doesn't pay.
- It takes seven "touches." At least seven.
- Find your strength and sell it.
- Find your weakness and defend it directly. Or admit your weakness and make it a strength.
- Exploit social media.
- Critique your performance.

- Learn from Trump.
- Look as good as you can.
- Speak with confidence.
- Highlight accomplishments.
- Raise the stakes.
- Promise good times.
- Fire on all cylinders. Take nothing for granted.
- Support the party; support other Democrats.

Democrats, like eagles, don't flock. We are fiercely independent in our thinking, so it can be challenging to get us to organize effectively. Contrast this with Republicans, who are notorious for marching in lockstep. In order to enjoy long-term success, the Democratic Party must present a party-wide, desirable, consistent, emotionally connected brand identity to future voters.

CHAPTER 4

DEFENDING THE DEMOCRATIC BRAND

Build a Swift and Potent "Strike Force"

In recent elections, there was talk about "rapid-response" teams, or a strike force. The goal was to respond quickly to lies and distortions leveled at our candidates.

What happened? Were Democrats too focused, again, on not offending anybody? Some campaigns made efforts to counteract direct attacks, but most failed to set up a reliable, effective strike force.

We need to punch back immediately. It's better to get low-production-value ads into the media quickly than no ad at all! And we need to also push out our side of the story via PR campaigns.

We have to stop letting Republicans get away with truth-twisting messages and blatant lies. Don't allow their charges to stick, to fester. Ignoring lies or distortions is a major marketing gaffe. When consumers believe a product—or candidate—is tarnished in some way, it becomes exceedingly difficult to reverse that perception.

Again, 1 or 2 percent swings can change everything, so we can never be complacent.

We must respond.

So we suggest the DNC, along with most other campaign groups, set up and fund a centralized strike force to immediately develop smart, sharp responses to all GOP attacks, with special emphasis on attacks that blatantly lie or distort reality. And their output should be sent to all involved—the candidates and their campaign teams as well as the press and social media influencers.

For years Republicans whipped us with less-qualified candidates than we had because they knew how, verbally, to get everyone on the same train. They all said the same potent phrases at every opportunity.

We need to do that too. It's time for all Democrats to seek and accept unified talking points. A centralized command post—perhaps coordinated by the DNC—to develop and disperse those talking points is vitally important.

Three Politicians Walk Into a Bar . . .

And while we are on the topic of responding assertively, we happily point out that Democrats have a weapon not generally available to Republicans: comedians. It's a fact that overwhelmingly the sharpest comedians, satirists, and certainly the late-night TV hosts lean left. Why let their barbs go to waste?

It would be wonderful if Democrats once in a while said things like, "As Stephen Colbert pointed out last night . . ."

Just don't overdo it. Professional comedians make comedy look easy. It's not. *Use sparingly*. And don't make the rookie mistake of saying something you think is funny and then waiting for the laugh. Just say the line, with a smile if appropriate, and move on. Barack Obama had the timing and delivery of a world-class comedian. His skill in front of a microphone was apparently innate. Too bad few others have that gene.

And we have plenty of other sources for top-level rejoinders. New Yorker satirist Andy Borowitz, the podcasters behind *Pod Save America*, the monologue writers of Joy Reid's show on MSNBC, and Trevor Noah's *The Daily Show*—all produce powerful punchlines on a regular basis.

Why not harvest that bounty? It's free—but be sure to give proper credit—and it's a tool Republicans lack. Just a small team could be tasked with mining the nightly nuggets and getting them out to Democrats frequently.

Making that a daily ritual would be best, since timeliness is vital.

Know Your Enemy

Every marketing pro will tell you: "Know your competition."

In the political arena, that means getting on their mailing lists. Watch right-wing media. Read at least some of what they read. There is nothing to be gained by being ignorant as to what the other side is saying about us. We cannot counteract what we don't know.

They have their hot-button issues, and some of those issues might be uncomfortable for you. Too bad. You must always be prepared for their most fraught topics: border security, abortion, violent demonstrations, and so on. You have to have succinct responses to whatever riles up the Right.

If you don't have the stomach for watching the propaganda spewing from Fox News or Newsmax, at least have one of your staff keep you up-to-date with the latest nonsense coming from their hosts and guests and the latest phrases they are using.

Change the Vocabulary

We need to change the language we use, and we need to add emotional connotations. Democrats need to implant these words—these *ideas*—in voters' minds:

Old	New
Regulations	Protections (all regulations are protections)
Gun control	Gun safety/commonsense gun laws
Global warming	Climate change (or better, climate crisis or emergency)
Pro-life	Anti-choice (No Dem should ever say "pro-life"), pro-forced birth
Liberal	Progressive
Entitlements	Earned benefits
Mainstream media	Free press
Elite	Smart, successful
Government handouts	Investments in the people
Defund the police	Reimagine policing
Bureaucrats	Dedicated public servants
Spending	Investing in America

Words matter, especially words that become images in the mind. Don't let Republicans own the political dictionary.

Rebrand Republicans

Over the past couple of decades, the GOP has learned the importance of local elections. They stayed on message, and they took over statehouses and redrew the districts. But we can stop their momentum. As we mentioned earlier, it's not just about building our brand; it's also about defining the opposition in relation to us.

Democrats should remind voters repeatedly:

- Republicans fight for corporations, not people.
- Republicans give tax cuts to millionaires and billionaires because that's where they get their biggest contributions.
- Republican politicians are in the pockets of the special interests: the NRA, Big Oil, the Koch brothers, Big Pharma, etc.
- Republican politicians don't care about *you*.
- Republicans refuse to accept responsibility for their actions. A total of 147 Republicans voted to overturn the 2020 election results. Not a single Republican voted for the 2021 COVID-19 relief package.
- *Republicans are the party of no: no health care plan, no infrastructure plan, no education plan, no save-the-planet plan*. Again and again, big corporations are prioritized ahead of people. Worse, they put the party ahead of the country.

If *every* Democratic candidate repeats those phrases whenever and wherever they fit, minds will change.

And not just candidates: all of us on the left have to send out the same message clearly and often.

Voters don't remember specific details about a speech or a debate, but targeted, emotionally charged phrases stick, especially when repeated frequently.

Call Extremists What They Are: Extremists

We need to remind voters that this ain't your daddy's GOP.

The Republican Party today bears little resemblance to the party of Eisenhower, Dole, or McCain. Now, thanks mostly to the pervasive influence of right-wing media, moderate Republicans are a dying breed. Conspiracy theory nut jobs, QAnon followers, white supremacists, and religious fanatics have a stranglehold on the party, and nowhere is that felt more than in the primary battles. As we pointed out earlier, this book is written for Democrats campaigning against Republicans, not Democrats battling each other in primaries.

The most vociferous right-wing extremists in Congress—Jim Jordan, Marjorie Taylor Greene, Lauren Boebert, Josh Hawley, Louie Gohmert, Paul Gosar, Mo Brooks, etc.—need to be called out at every opportunity. These people, with their bizarre theories and wild accusations, are termites gnawing at the foundations of democracy. They are not funny; they are not harmless. They are dangerous and should not be ignored by Democrats.

Sometimes it seems as though Republicans do a better job at calling out the fanatics than we do—albeit out-of-office Republicans like George W. Bush, John Boehner, Joe Scarborough, John Kasich, or out-of-the-spotlight Republican thought leaders like George Will, Max Boot, or David Frum. These self-described conservatives seethe at what's become of their formerly *Grand* Old Party.

So let's start saying "extremists," or perhaps even better, "radical," when talking about the Far Right. Because that is what they are.

But in many cases that's still not going far enough. As long as the "Moderate Right" is appeasing the "Far Right," it's fair to use the word *extremist* when talking about the GOP as a whole. If they as a party kneel to the extremist fringe of their party, they should be saddled with that label as well.

Keep in mind: When 147 Republicans vote to overturn the results of an American election, *despite no evidence of fraud*, and when every modest policy proposal of every Democratic politician is called "socialist," terms like, *wingnut*, *crackpot*, and good old *fanatic* all become fair descriptors of the current GOP. Even *the lunatic fringe*, when it's appropriate.

Feel free to use those terms. They earned it.

But in terms of overall branding, we suggest this tactic: Let's rebrand Republicans as the party of the "radical Right." This should be a key phrase that we repeat often so that it burrows into the minds of voters and gets attached to all Republicans. The alliteration doesn't hurt either.

And finally, when we hear a sitting member of Congress compare lifesaving mask mandates with what Jews faced during the Holocaust, feel free to label her and any of her cohorts *unhinged* or *deranged*.

We need to forcefully call out those who so obviously deserve mockery and disdain.

Build *their* brand. Make the public see them for what they are. They are the radical Right.

Being coy gets us nowhere.

Even the Leaders Are Now *Radical Right* Republicans

That's not an exaggeration. And it gets worse every single day.

On June 29, 2021, House Minority Leader Kevin McCarthy tweeted:

"Democrats are desperate to pretend their party has progressed from their days of supporting slavery, pushing Jim Crow laws, and supporting the KKK.

"But today, the Dem Party has simply replaced the racism

of the Klan with the racism of Critical Race Theory."[*]

Everything about this tweet is intensely wrong, insulting, and just plain empty-headed. Not one thing he says there makes any sense. But anyone who peeks inside the right-wing media bubble knows this is exactly the type of repulsive attack millions of Americans are seeing, hearing, and reading daily from Republican leaders. And you know when the sharp lurch to the right accelerated—yes, with the worst president ever.

How can we have serious policy discussions when radical Right Republicans live on an alternate planet where truth and facts are optional?

We can't. Our only alternative is to forcefully, passionately, and repeatedly call out their dangerous and fact-free nonsense.

Be Offensive

You, the Democratic candidate, are on the right side of history. Don't cede *any* topic. There is not one area of American life that would be improved under Republicans.

Instead, for a change, put Republicans on defense. *Make them defend their often indefensible positions.*

---

[*] Kevin McCarthy (@GOPLeader), "Democrats are desperate to pretend their party has progressed from their days of supporting slavery, pushing Jim Crow laws, and supporting the KKK," Twitter, June 29, 2021, 3:29 p.m., https://twitter.com/gopleader/status/1409957285816897537.

Here are five to get you started.

1. Dark Money

During the 2020 presidential primaries, Governor Steve Bullock of Montana told NBC News that his number-one campaign issue was dark money. He tried to articulate the dangers of unbridled funds coming into campaigns from hidden sources. But for many reasons, his campaign foundered, and so that message never gained traction.

But it should. This is a vital issue that Democrats can and should push on, hard. Thankfully, a few—too few—Democrats have joined the fight.

From Senator Sheldon Whitehouse's website, April 11, 2019:

> *Washington, D.C.* – U.S. Senator Sheldon Whitehouse (D-RI) today introduced the DISCLOSE Act of 2019, which would require organizations spending money in federal elections to disclose their donors and help guard against hidden foreign interference in American democracy.*

---

* "Sheldon Whitehouse - United States Senator for Rhode Island," Sheldon Whitehouse - United States Senator for Rhode Island (U.S. Senate, April 11, 2019), https://www.whitehouse.senate.gov/news/release/whitehouse-introduces-disclose-act-to-restore-americans-trust-in-democracy.

Dark money is killing our democracy. That is not hyperbole. Dark money contaminates every corner of American politics. It's not a hot issue, because Democrats have not made it a hot issue. Let's change that.

Here's what we'd love to see in a debate:

> "Senator Grassley, you and I both accept campaign money from various sources. But I support a bill that lets the voters know exactly *who* gave us the money. You opposed that. Why? Are you ashamed of your donors? Do you not think voters have a right to know that you might have a conflict of interest when you take any particular position? Why do you want to keep the voters in the dark? *What are you hiding?*"

And if "dark money" seems too much of a political phrase, call it *hidden money* or *secret money*.

2. Tax Inequities

You know what Republicans—and Independents and Democrats, but especially Republicans—hate? People who rip off the government. Tax dollars being spent on people who don't "deserve" our help.

And they feel strongly about it because for their entire lives they've seen and heard examples of it in the right-wing media. Remember "Welfare queens"? More on this later under "Case Study: The "Welfare State."

Of course, what they don't see are *the much bigger rip-offs* perpetrated by people at the top of the pyramid.

Donald Trump, to name one ostentatious example, lives like a potentate, with gold splashed throughout his apartments, including his gold-plated toilet. You know, like any "populist." Yet his tax returns show him losing hundreds of millions of dollars year after year. And as a result, he paid pitifully little or nothing for many years.

And as we learned in early June 2021, in an explosive report from ProPublica ("The Secret IRS Files: Trove of Never-Before-Seen Records Reveal How the Wealthiest Avoid Income Tax"), the twenty-five richest Americans, including Jeff Bezos, Michael Bloomberg, Carl Icahn, and Elon Musk, also paid little—and sometimes nothing—in federal income taxes between 2014 and 2018.[*]

Which means we, the American taxpayer, subsidize their lifestyles. We give them the police departments to protect their buildings and golf courses, the armed services to ensure

---

[*] Jeff Ernsthausen, Paul Kiel, and Jesse Eisinger, "The Secret IRS Files: Trove of Never-before-Seen Records Reveal How the Wealthiest Avoid Income Tax," ProPublica, June 8, 2021, https://www.propublica.org/article/the-secret-irs-files-trove-of-never-before-seen-records-reveal-how-the-wealthiest-avoid-income-tax.

domestic and international tranquility, the roads and ports to ship their goods, the education system to ensure a steady supply of literate employees.

Where is the anger, the outrage of the little guy being ripped off?

Where are the Democrats saying those people are playing all of us for suckers?

It's nowhere because Democrats let it slide. We gave them a free pass.

Why?

Trump and those billionaires are simply the most visible examples of the major tax inequities built into the American tax code, yet people who are offended by a college student begging for loan forgiveness look the other way when Trump and his cohorts write off millions of dollars in questionable business expenses. This is a major Democratic failing. We haven't pounded the drum loudly enough about this side of the story.

The superwealthy need to *pay their fair share*. Right now, they don't. Democrats need to make the phrase "pay your fair share" part of America's consciousness.

Clearly, "Let's make the tax system fair" is a winning issue.

"Pay your fair share!" resonates. It's visceral. It connects with voters. Plus, who could argue against that?

Well, Republicans can and do. And they will look foolish and mean.

3. Tax Cheats

An unfair tax system is bad enough. Even worse, by a few degrees, are the people who blatantly scam the system.

No one likes a cheater, and there is special enmity for wealthy tax cheaters. Yet America is awash in one-percenters who, through guile and expensive advisors, pay little or nothing to support America's needs.

Want specifics? Search for "Shrinking the Tax Gap: A Comprehensive Approach." This eye-opening November 2020 study by a former IRS commissioner, law professor, and former secretary of the treasury—Charles Rossotti, Natasha Sarin, and Lawrence Summers, respectively—will get your blood boiling.

It turns out the money lost by not enforcing our tax rules fairly would immediately change the calculus for virtually all important legislation.

The authors say, "Over the course of the next decade, barring changes in tax administration efforts, we can expect to lose an estimated $7.5 trillion, or around 3 percent of GDP, annually that our existing law should allow us to collect."[*]

And this as well:

---

[*] Charles O Rossotti, Natasha Sarin, and Lawrence H Summers, "Shrinking the Tax Gap: A Comprehensive Approach," Tax Notes Federal, November 30, 2020, https://shrinkthetaxgap.com/shrinking-the-tax-gap-november-30-2020/.

> Over the last 25 years IRS funding has been steadily cut ... Faced with fewer resources, the IRS has pulled back from enforcement efforts across the board, with the most precipitous drop for high earners ... Audit rates for the top 1 percent have fallen so significantly that those earners are as likely to face IRS scrutiny as are individuals claiming the earned income tax credit.

And finally this: "By conservative estimates $1 spent on IRS enforcement returns $12 in additional tax revenue collected."[*]

These findings are nowhere in the current political consciousness, yet they can be red meat for Democrats and Independents. But they can only become fuel if we light the fire.

And to be clear, it's not that these wealthy tax cheats are "smart" because they figured out how to game the system. We can't allow Republicans to reframe them that way. They are *tax cheaters*, and we should call them that.

Former Australian prime minister Malcolm Turnbull, writing in *Time* (August 23, 2021) summarized it perfectly:

"We can debate whether tax rates should be higher or lower—but not whether taxes are optional. If everybody

---

[*] Ibid.

pays, then everybody can pay less."*

Along with *pay your fair share*, going after high-income tax cheats should be a no-brainer, long-term branding issue for Democrats.

4. Income Inequality

The statistics get worse every year, yet the only solutions Republicans offer are more tax cuts for the wealthy. But *why* tax cuts for the wealthy? "A rising economic tide lifts all boats," they tell us in lockstep.

To which we should reply, "Under your system, only the mega-yachts are rising!"

All the dinghies, rowboats, and fishing trawlers—the "boats" of the working class—are at the same level as they were decades ago.

According to *Deloitte Insights* blog of July 2020:

> In the past 30 years, the proportion of wealth held by those in the top 10% of household income has risen from 60.8% to 70.0%. But even more remarkably, the wealth owned by just the top 1% of income earners has gone up

---

* Malcolm Turnbull, "How a New Deal for Global Taxation Might Save Democracy," *Time*, August 11, 2021, https://time.com/6084170/global-tax-ation-new-deal/.

from 17.2% to 26.8%—meaning that more than a quarter of the country's wealth is in the hands of the top 1%.*

How many more years will Democrats allow the GOP to take care of their own while ignoring the working men and women of America?

5. It's a Climate *Emergency*

One picture covered the entire front page of the "Sunday Review" section of the August 29, 2021, *New York Times*. It was a head-on shot of the Hoover Dam and splayed across the page, the only words to be seen were: **"Forty million people rely on the Colorado River. It's drying up fast**."†

In New York, on September 1, 2021, more than three inches of rain fell in a single hour in Central Park from the "remnants" of Hurricane Ida. That deluge shattered the previous record, one that had been set just ten days earlier by Tropical Storm Henri.

---

* "COVID-19's Impact on US Income Inequality: It's Going to Get Worse before It Gets Better," *Deloitte Insights* (blog), July 23, 2020, https://www2.deloitte.com/us/en/insights/economy/issues-by-the-numbers/covid-19-impact-on-income-inequality.html.

† Abrahm Lustgarten, "40 Million People Rely on the Colorado River. It's Drying Up Fast.," *New York Times*, August 27, 2021, https://www.nytimes.com/2021/08/27/sunday-review/colorado-river-drying-up.html.

Climate change *is* an emergency. Schoolkids know it. Europeans know it. The United Nations has been screaming about it for years. And climate scientists around the world warn us daily.

On just a single day in mid-August 2021, we saw millions of acres burning on the West Coast, people drowning in Carolina floods, huge tropical storms heading for the East Coast, along with long-standing drought in the midlands and the Southwest.

Once-in-a-hundred-year events now occur with frightening regularity.

Strangely, the truth is that most Republican *voters* know it. But GOP politicians either deny the reality of the climate crisis or they grudgingly accept it as true but drag their feet on any legislation that will help reverse the looming cataclysm.

This is an issue that Democrats *own*. Business as usual—being polite or quiet—accomplishes nothing. Few if any Republicans can speak with full-throated passion about their attempts to fix the climate calamity. On the other hand, just about every Democrat anywhere can say, at the very least, "I fully support laws that will protect your planet. Your air. Your water!"

We have to call it what it is: a *climate emergency. It's a climate crisis.* It's not some far-off idea about the distant future or about protecting polar bears. We are feeling its effects today, and people are dying because of it. Recycling campaigns and banning plastic straws won't make the difference we need. It requires large-scale international efforts. The United States can and should take the lead, and Democrats are the ones to do it.

As the cliché says, we have only one Earth. There is no planet B.

It's way past time for Democrats to pound the table about the real and present danger we face; it's time to make climate change a front-burner issue. Politicians who are in the pockets of the fossil fuel industry can no longer be tolerated.

This is an issue that young people care deeply about. Show them that we are the party willing to take a stand and make real change. Do it because it will take these voters off the sidelines and onto our side.

Democrats are the Green Party in America. Embrace that. Explain the huge short- and long-term benefits.

At the same time, brand Republicans as climate change deniers. Brand them as anti-science. Get the populace riled up about dark and dirty water, soil, and air.

Otherwise, in the not-distant future, our planet—our home—will be unrecognizable. And uninhabitable.

Make Republicans Pay for Their Actions

As a Democrat, you surely agree that Republicans do more bad things than our team does. When their actions are particularly egregious, it behooves us to remind the public, repeatedly.

Three examples we can keep bringing up:

1. George W. Bush and his Republican team lied about weapons of mass destruction. Those lies caused Congress, Republicans and Democrats alike, to authorize the war, which was terribly costly in both dollars, and more importantly, American lives. Not to mention a frighteningly severe recession as GWB left office.

2. When it came time for Congress to certify the 2020 election, an astonishing 147 Republicans voted to overturn the election results. This is America, not some third-world dictatorship! The case that the election results were accurate is beyond question. Republicans voting against the will of the people is an unconscionable attack on the bedrock of our democracy.

3. While still in the midst of the COVID-19 pandemic, with its concurrent severe economic downturn, not one Congressional Republican voted for the rescue package. Not one, even though all polls showed Americans overwhelmingly wanted the bill to pass. Democrats should beat the crap out of them on this one issue alone!

When Republicans clearly act against the best interests of Americans, Democrats must continually remind voters of what happened. Not casually, not in passing, not when the subject comes up. Candidates must pounce on every opportunity to tarnish the opposition, just like they do to us!

Politics isn't pretty. Play hardball.

Label Republican Lies as Lies

Republicans lie more than us. They lie without guilt, and they have lied for decades. Trump is merely the latest and most over-the-top iteration. Overall, they have been heavily rewarded for their duplicity.

On the other hand, *we* have paid the price for being the good guys.

The only way to reverse that is to attack their lies head-on. Swiftly and repeatedly.

Make them pay for their lies. Don't play games with words. Don't say "falsehood" or "misleading" or "misrepresentation" or any other polite, inoffensive term when talking about lies. Say, "That's a lie," when it really is. Say, "She's lying," when you are certain that is what she is doing. Voters respond to blunt statements more than subtle innuendo.

Use Republicans to Fight Our Battles

It's good when we attack Republicans. It's *much better* when Republicans attack Republicans.

There's this mind-boggling fact: some of the strongest attacks leveled against Donald Trump came out of the mouths of Republicans, yet Democrats squandered the resulting marketing opportunities that fell in their lap.

During the 2016 primaries, Ted Cruz, Mitt Romney, and Lindsey Graham all smeared Donald Trump with words Democrats could barely dream of.

Cruz: "This man is a pathological liar. He doesn't know the difference between truth and lies. He lies practically every word that comes out of his mouth, and in a pattern that I think is straight out of a psychology textbook, his response is to accuse everybody else of lying. The man is utterly amoral."[*]

Romney: "Donald Trump is a phony, a fraud. His promises are as worthless as a degree from Trump University."[†]

Graham: "He's a race-baiting, xenophobic, religious bigot."[‡]

---

[*] Tina Nguyen, "'Pathological Liar': Ted Cruz Unloads in Epic Rant after Trump Accuses His Father of Helping J.F.K.'s Assassin," *Vanity Fair*, May 3, 2016, https://www.vanityfair.com/news/2016/05/ted-cruz-donald-trump-jfk-liar.

[†] Mitt Romney (speech, Utah, Salt Lake City, March 3, 2016), https://www.washingtonpost.com/news/post-politics/wp/2016/03/03/mitt-romney-trump-is-a-phony-a-fraud-who-is-playing-the-american-public-for-suckers)/.

[‡] "Episode 12/8/2015," in *New Day*, CNN, December 8, 2015.

So there we have explosive, high-octane ammunition—"expert testimony" against the Republican candidate from high-profile Republicans. What did Democrats do with these right-wing attacks against Trump?

Almost nothing.

These GOP-born attacks against Trump were gold-tipped arrows, but alas, they remained stuck in our quiver.

Infomercials fully appreciate the unequaled power of testimonials. There are thousands of infomercials on television, past and present, and every one of them uses testimonials to make the case for their product. What you say about yourself or your product or your candidate is always less effective than what some third person says. Democrats, for some reason, have mostly chosen to ignore testimonials that were there for the taking.

We must never again be so blind to such powerful campaign gifts.

Discover and Exploit Hot-Button Topics

Starting in 2018, the best issue for Democrats became health care. Most of us knew that was the case, but too often our candidates let themselves be sidetracked into discussions of less-hot issues. Fight that tendency.

Mentally prepare. Remind yourself of what one or two

points you *must* make during every rally, every town hall, every interview. Get your staff to understand that part of their job is to remind you.

And remind voters that while Republicans in Congress voted dozens of times to repeal the Affordable Care Act, they *never* offered a full-blown plan of their own. Nor did Trump, despite his repeated assurances that his "beautiful" replacement plan was just weeks away from completion.

Every person needs health care. Remind them that we have a system that allows millions of Americans to fall through the cracks every year, and next year it could be them. Bernie Sanders has the script for this: no candidate needs to reinvent the wheel. He'll be happy (we assume!) to allow other left-leaning candidates to help with his quest.

But naturally, the hot-button issue of the day will change over time. That's what polls are for. Watch for trending topics that consistently appear on top of a variety of polls.

Here are some other topics that Republicans have branded for their own purposes.

Case Study: Patriotism

Are Republicans more patriotic than Democrats? Of course not! But they wear their lapel pins; they wave their flags. And we let them "own" patriotism.

Here's how bad it's become: In the summer of 2021, a left-leaning Long Island farmer was hassled by Democrats who assumed that because he painted a large American flag on the side of the barn at his farm stand that he must be a right-winger. That's nuts. Republicans absolutely do not love the flag, or any other true symbol of patriotism, more than we do.

Let's fight back on this. We need to retake the long-held patina of patriotism from the Right. We need to stress that there are more registered Democrats than Republicans. Therefore, Democrats *are* America.

We should point out that many, many military veterans run for office as Democrats. Many retired admirals and generals actively support Democrats. We need to remind voters that Republicans implicitly defended the murderous mob of insurrectionists who attacked the Capitol on January 6, 2021. Those bloodthirsty traitors were there specifically to stop the most precious moment of American democracy: the peaceful transition of power.

In fact, Democrats love America *more* than Republicans because we believe in the *ideals* of America, not merely the bumper-sticker slogans of the Right.

Say that. Bend the brand recognition about patriotism away from Republicans and toward Democrats.

And let's start putting these words:

into our flyers, onto our yard signs, and into our marketing. Let's bake our patriotism directly into our branding.

Let it be known that Democrats are the party of *real* patriotism.

Case Study: Abortion

As mentioned under "Change the Vocabulary," no Democrat should ever use the term *pro-life* to describe the other side. We are pro-choice; they are anti-choice. *They are no-choice.*

And we fight to improve the lives of children after they are born. We fight for health care, childcare, early education, and food security. We fight against Republicans who typically refuse to allocate money to protect the baby once she or he comes into the world, saying, in effect, "You're on your own, kid."

And you might also point out, "All birth control methods fail at some point. Would you accept the government forcing you to have a child you truly don't want?"

When abortion is outlawed—or made difficult to obtain— the result is one of three possible outcomes:

1. Women will seek, as they always have, illegal abortions. Some will be safe, and some will cause the woman irreparable harm. Or death.

2. The fetus is carried to term, and the child is given up for adoption. For some, that may be a choice, but for many others, for many reasons, that process becomes highly problematic, i.e. children with special needs or children of color ("The US adoption system discriminates against darker-skinned children.")[*]

3. The baby is born to a woman who wanted an abortion but could not afford one or couldn't find a provider in her state. And that baby, by definition, is an *unwanted child*. Which is obviously and deeply tragic, but there are untold variations of women (fourteen-year-olds who were coerced into sex; single mothers living in poverty; families struggling with more children than they can handle; mothers who are told early on that the fetus has a massive, life-threatening deformity) for whom being forced to carry to term is itself dangerous and life-changing in a wrenching, negative way.

---

[*] Ronald Hall, "The US Adoption System Discriminates against Darker-skinned Children," The Conversation, February 21, 2019, https://theconversation.com/the-us-adoption-system-discriminates-against-darker-skinned-children-110976.

Abortion will always be a fraught, emotional issue, but ultimately it's an intensely private matter. Our candidates, however, should always stand firm, knowing that most Americans agree with the Democratic stance.

Start proclaiming yourself as proudly on the side of American women, American children, and American families. Don't cede an inch of this to Republicans, who are clearly out-of-step with the majority of the American public.

And finally, we'll include the following text that has been bouncing around the internet for a while (author unknown). It does a good job at humanizing the agony women in every city and town have faced or will face.

I'm not pro-abortion.

- I'm pro-Becky, who found out at her twenty-week anatomy scan that the infant she had been so excited to bring into this world had developed without life-sustaining organs.
- I'm pro-Susan, who was sexually assaulted on her way home from work, only to come to the horrific realization that her assailant planted his seed in her when she got a positive pregnancy test result a month later.
- I'm pro-Theresa, who hemorrhaged due to a placental abruption, causing her parents, spouse, and children

to have to make the impossible decision on whether to save her or her unborn child.

- I'm pro–little Cathy, who had her innocence ripped away from her by someone she should have been able to trust, and her eleven-year-old body isn't mature enough to bear the consequence of that betrayal.

- I'm pro-Melissa, who's working two jobs just to make ends meet and has to choose between bringing another child into poverty or feeding the children she already has because her spouse walked out on her.

- I'm pro-Brittany, who realizes that she is in no way financially, emotionally, or physically able to raise a child.

- I'm pro-Emily, who went through IVF, ending up with *six* viable implanted eggs requiring selective reduction to ensure the safety of her and a safe number of fetuses.

- I'm pro-Jessica, who *is finally* getting the strength to get away from her physically abusive spouse, only to find out she is carrying the monster's child.

- I'm pro-Vanessa, who went into her confirmation appointment *after years* of trying to conceive, only to hear silence where there should be a heartbeat.

- I'm pro-Lindsay, who lost her virginity in her sophomore year with a broken condom and now has to choose whether to be a teenage mom or just a teenager.

- I'm pro-Courtney, who just found out she's already thirteen weeks along, but the egg never made it out of her fallopian tube, so either she terminates the pregnancy or risks dying from internal bleeding.
- You can argue and say that I'm pro-choice all you want, but the truth is, I am pro-life. Their lives. Women's lives.

You don't get to pick and choose which scenarios should be accepted. It's not about which stories you don't agree with. It's about fighting for the women in the stories and the *choice* they have to make.

Women's rights are meant to *protect all* women, regardless of their situation!

And in light of the horrendous anti-choice legislation passed in late August 2021 by Texas—which will surely be emulated, with the approval of a stacked Supreme Court, by radical Right Republicans everywhere—the need for Democrats to act decisively has never been more urgent.

Case Study: "Job Creators"

You have heard it forever. It is the mantra of conservatives: "We must give tax breaks to the wealthy so they can create more jobs."

Nonsense! A quick Google search will yield dozens of

articles and studies to disprove this long-held GOP stance. One of the best, updated on October 10, 2017, comes from the Center on Budget and Policy Priorities, a respected non-partisan research and policy institute. The headline reads:

"Large Job Growth Unlikely to Follow Tax Cuts for the Rich and Corporations."*

Aside from the scholarly studies, there is common sense. I (Ken) have been a financial advisor for decades. In the thousands of conversations I've had with business owners over those years, I've never had a single person say or even hint that they won't hire new employees because of the prevailing tax laws. A few dollars more or less does not affect their hiring decisions in any meaningful ways.

Plus, tax cuts for the wealthy cast a wide net and reward all manner of fat cats—lawyers, investors, bankers, etc.—who have little or absolutely nothing to do with hiring decisions. Hiring depends on consumption, demand, and production. It rarely depends on whether a company gets a tax cut.

It's quite simple, really: the firm either needs that job done,

---

* Center on Budget and Policy Priorities, "Large Job Growth Unlikely to Follow Tax Cuts for the Rich and Corporations," Center on Budget and Policy Priorities, October 10, 2017, https://www.cbpp.org/research/federal-tax/large-job-growth-unlikely-to-follow-tax-cuts-for-the-rich-and-corporations.

or it doesn't. The prevailing tax rate is almost never in the conversation.

All of which means it is now time for Democrats to push back hard on the myths surrounding tax cuts for "job creators."

Case Study: Critical Race Theory

Ask your somewhat politically aware left-leaning friend about critical race theory, and they will likely—as of mid-2021, at least—stare back at you quizzically.

Now ask your Fox News–watching uncle. Not only will he know "all about it" but he will tell you why it's an insidious plot by "the radical leftist Democrats" to indoctrinate America's youth.

CRT, as it's known to the Right, is rarely mentioned on MSNBC—the exception is below—or CNN, and it's almost invisible on the nightly network news shows.

But seemingly out of nowhere, critical race theory became *a big thing* for Republicans. As Joy Reid so deliciously showed in detail on her MSNBC show, a small group planned this as a wedge issue, and they are executing it perfectly, having Republicans say the same thing everywhere, over and over.

CRT has been around since the 1970s. There is no widespread, unified Democratic plan to push CRT within our schools. But some discussion about racism and other forms of discrimination is always desirable.

The current dustup seems to have started with conservative activist Christopher Rufo. His repeated use of the term propelled the controversy into the mainstream. In particular, one infamous tweet of his seemed to push the ball down the hill: "The goal is to have the public read something crazy in the newspaper and immediately think 'critical race theory.'"*

Aha! So there we have it. He said the quiet thing out loud.

Republicans always make issues like this a cultural thing because they know they can't win on a policy argument. Hence, Fox News is all agog about Dr. Seuss, Mr. Potato Head, cancel culture, etc. You know, the really important stuff.

Democrats need to know what the GOP is saying and be prepared to push back.

Case Study: Trickle-Down Economics

You should know and proclaim that many of the GOP's talking points about economics are pure bunk. And trickle-down economics is a prime example. It posits that keeping

---

* Christopher F. Rufo (@realchrisrufo), "The goal is to have the public read something crazy in the newspaper and immediately think "critical race theory," Twitter, March 15, 2021, 3:17 p.m., https://twitter.com/realchrisrufo/status/1371541044592996352?s=20.

the rich, well, rich—primarily by using tax cuts—allows their wealth to trickle down to everyone else.

It sounds somewhat plausible, but it's a dubious notion disputed by economists. For example, here's a succinct tidbit from Nobel Prize–winning economist Paul Krugman, writing on June 1, 2021, in the *New York Times*: "Predictions that tax cuts will produce economic miracles have never panned out—not once. Neither, by the way, have predictions that tax hikes, like the increased levees on corporations and the wealthy that Biden is proposing, will lead to disaster."[*]

Got that? Trickle-down economics doesn't work! Period. Krugman, among many others, has explained this in detail many times, in many places. And time and time again the US economy did just fine after tax hikes.

Trickle-down economics ensures the superwealthy stay secure atop the economic pyramid while doing little or nothing for everyone else. Republicans, for generations, have shown themselves to be pro-*upward* transfer of wealth. They are the reverse Robin Hood! They take from the poor and middle class and ensure the fat cats stay fat. Or get fatter.

Say that!

---

[*] Paul Krugman, "The Radical Modesty of Biden's Budget," *New York Times*, May 31, 2021, https://www.nytimes.com/2021/05/31/opinion/biden-budget-proposal.html.

Case Study: Deficit Spending

Just about every Republican politician harps on the idea that "we can't keep spending away our children's future." As do some Democrats. (See: Manchin, Joe.) Ronald Reagan compared our national spending to a home mortgage, a debt "everyone knows must be paid down." But these are false analogies and make no sense. Home mortgages almost always have a specific end date; sovereign debt does not. Homeowners cannot print new money; the United States government can.

Most importantly, however, is that our children and subsequent generations can do exactly what we've been doing—that is, pass the debt on to the next generation. *There is no due date for national debt.*

Yes, demographics will muddy up this scenario somewhat, but the main point is that when we have a clear need to spend—a war, a pandemic, crumbling infrastructure—we should spend.

And we especially should spend—or more correctly, *invest*—when we can borrow at historically low interest rates, which is what we have now and are likely to have for some time ahead. That is precisely what smart businesspeople do, and governments can and should do the same.

Democrats need to stop allowing the GOP to perpetuate their false narrative about deficit spending, and we do it by branding that narrative as *false*. Because it is.

Case Study: The "Welfare State"

Few things rankle the brains of Republicans more than the idea that some people, "the takers," get free money from "the makers." Also see: *freeloaders*, *moochers*, *parasites*, *deadbeats*. The slurs change; the perceptions don't.

Let's dive into this morass and see how Democrats ought to frame that issue.

The Reagan-era vision of the "welfare queen" loading up her cart with cigarettes, cheap wine, and junk food still persists, albeit less overtly than in the past. It all fits neatly into the perception that "those people"—and yes, there is definitely a racial overtone to this—are a drag on the hard workers we all know and love.

Of course, no one wants to see people cheat the system. But there is a major fallacy in that welfare state line of thinking: it misses the fact that there are *two* types of "welfare" in America, and one type—when the rich get *corporate* welfare—is overlooked and much more destructive to our society.

Here's a particularly incendiary example: When, for whatever reason, a low-level drug dealer gets a check from the government, that lawbreaker still needs to eat and sleep somewhere. Meaning, his "welfare" money will, directly or indirectly, be spent *in the community* for food, shelter, clothing, cars, or yes, more drugs. But eventually, *all* his government money filters through the local shops and service providers. And those shop owners and service providers pay taxes.

Now let's jump to the other extreme. And let's use Mitt Romney as the example. When he ran for president in 2012, his tax returns showed (remember when *all* presidential candidates released their returns?) that his most recent tax rate was around 14 percent. That's incredibly low for someone as wealthy as Mitt, and it's especially low being that he knew the public would see those returns one day. Even worse, tax experts said at the time he probably could have gotten them down to 10 percent if he wanted to be superaggressive. But thanks to high-paid lobbyists and the best tax lawyers and accountants, Mitt kept his multimillions for himself. Did his extra money find its way to the local bodega? Not much of it did. We found out that he kept lots of his cash stashed away in off-shore accounts—just like tens of thousands of his superwealthy buddies.

So it's a true statement that the drug dealers and the Mitt Romneys of America each took advantage of the government's largess, but only one side of the equation—the lowly drug dealers—turns almost all their income into tax revenues that help pay for schools, cops, teachers, soldiers, and roads. The fat cats count on the rest of us to pick up the tab.

Untold numbers of industries, from giant corporate farming to earth-ravaging mining operators, are all recipients of corporate welfare. And as a few people in Congress have continually tried to point out, the Pentagon spends—or wastes—billions on failed projects, but every time they do the contractors still walk away with immense rewards. And no one seems to say a word about it.

The mother who gets government assistance to help feed her four kids is scorned, while the tax-dodging, corporate welfare–getting CEO with four homes is admired—by some.

Over the past decades, Republicans successfully turned our eyes and our outrage onto the so-called "takers," and Democrats let them get away with it. At the same time, Democrats failed miserably to stoke righteous outrage and resentment against the real takers: those who have the means to help our country prosper but choose to keep it locked away.

This has been branding malfeasance. We need to more vigorously channel voters' resentment away from the struggling economically disadvantaged and toward the smug men and women who want us to believe they deserve to keep their prodigious wealth more or less intact.

The vast majority of recipients of government assistance are good people, and Democrats know that money spent on helping them is an investment in our shared future.

Say that.

Case Study: Defund the Police

In the classic Mel Brooks and Thomas Meehan Broadway musical *The Producers*, the get-rich-quick scheme concocted by the "heroes" of the story required a show that was guaranteed to flop.

In politics, it would be hard to imagine a more surefire phrase to attain failure for Democrats than *Defund the Police*.

To be clear, "Defund the Police" was never a party slogan; it was a product of fervent public outcry from one aggrieved segment of society. Nonetheless, right-wing media jumped on it and wanted voters to believe that every Democrat wanted to shut down their local police department.

We all understand the underlying ethos of the defund movement. It grew out of the anger of the horrendous George Floyd murder, when passions predictably reached a boiling point. And in truth, most defunders did not advocate literally abolishing their hometown police departments. But to the general voting public, that's what it sounded like!

As usual, the Republicans were all over it, and also as usual, Democrats were painfully slow to set the record straight—if they responded at all.

Many, if not most, Democrats agree that changes in policing are needed. But the slogans should have been along the lines of . . .

- Reorganize the Police
- Free the Police to Do Policing
- Better Police, Safer Neighborhoods

The voters who decide tight elections want to be assured that they live in a safe neighborhood. They want to know that if they need the police, competent, well-trained professionals will respond quickly. "Defund the Police" requires a full explanation, but only a tiny minority of the population will give even a minute to researching the plans behind the slogan.

Democrats must not let Republicans win on this! We must respond quickly, or the law and order issue will again work against us. We know that Democrats want safe streets as much as anyone else.

Say that! Only after you have made that clear can you proceed to explain how you propose to reform the police.

Case Study: Voter Fraud

It's so easy for Democrats to tar Republicans with the "Big Lie." But after some time, that phrase will become just one more weed on the political landscape—attention-getting for a moment, then unnoticed by anyone.

We all know that "widespread voter fraud" is itself a

fraudulent statement. Democrats can and should swat it away by having a few retorts at the ready:

1. Ask a Big Lie liar, "How many cases did you guys win in court? Not only did you not succeed in getting courts to take you seriously but many of the cases were thrown out, sometimes by Trump-appointed judges, with disdain and derision."

2. If there was fraud, why did Democrats lose so many seats in the House? (Or the corollary, "Why did the 'fraud perpetrators' let so many Republicans win *but not Trump*?")

3. Why has there never, not once, been a proven case of widespread outcome-shifting voter fraud?

Then, too, there is just plain common sense. Who in the world would stand in line for any length of time to cast an illegal vote—*one* illegal vote—knowing he or she could be jailed for that action? That alone is hard to fathom, and it's backed up by every serious investigation ever done because it simply makes no sense.

Every American who personally knows a poll worker knows our system is chock-full with checks and balances at every step of the way. We are the envy of the world when it comes to ensuring free, fair, and honest elections.

The phony voter fraud claims are one of the worst remnants of Trumpism. Today's Republicans should be made to pay for their horrendous nonstop lies. The press can only do so much. It's up to Democrats to brand Republicans as the Anti-America Party because they now work to destroy many of our most precious and most basic values.

Case Study: Benghazi

To this day, Republicans chant, "Lock her up!" at the slightest provocation. The riotous chanters will tell you with smug certainty that Hillary Clinton committed all manner of heinous deeds. Chief among them, they claim with certainty, was her role in the death of four Americans in the 2012 attack on two United States government facilities in Benghazi, Libya.

Why do Republican rally-goers feel that antagonism toward the former secretary of state? It's because their congressional leaders and right-wing media fanned those flames incessantly for years.

But here's what they do not know:

The matter was investigated thoroughly—an astonishing ten investigations in all—and beyond any doubt, Secretary Clinton did nothing wrong. That's not a partisan opinion.

Specifically, the allegations were looked into by an independent board commissioned by the State Department, the

FBI, two Democrat-controlled Senate committees, and, most importantly in terms of politics, *six* Republican-controlled House committees.

Democrats must know this: After the first *five* Republican investigations found no evidence of wrongdoing by any senior Obama administration official, in 2014 House Republicans opened that sixth investigation! You likely recall the sparks generated by the House Select Committee on Benghazi, chaired by rowdy Trey Gowdy. That committee, which finagled national gavel-to-gavel television and radio coverage, grilled Secretary Clinton for eleven hours. She remained calm and in control throughout, yet for some reason little of her steadfast performance that day appeared on the evening news.

In the end, Gowdy sheepishly admitted they were unable—again!—to find any evidence of wrongdoing by Ms. Clinton or any other senior Obama administration official.

Then, on September 29, 2015, Republican House majority leader Kevin McCarthy, who was at the time trying to become Speaker of the House, told Sean Hannity on Fox News that, "Everybody thought Hillary Clinton was unbeatable, right? But we put together a Benghazi special committee, a select committee. What are her (poll) numbers today? Her numbers are dropping."*

---

* "September 29, 2015," in *Hannity*, Fox News, September 29, 2015.

So there you have it. A full admission: they wasted time and taxpayer money on those multiple hearings purely for political gain. What price did the GOP pay for those costly shenanigans? Nothing! Why? Because again, Democrats allowed Republicans to seize the branding message. Despite the fact that Benghazi, as a political issue, should be a faded dot in the rearview mirror, it remains a rallying cry at any large GOP gathering. Worse, they—or Russian bots—have now begun to paint Joe Biden with the Benghazi brush. There are social media memes floating around in 2021 asking, "Who was the vice president when four Americans died?"

That dark, baseless trope is affecting millions of voters. Democrats need to quash it to set the record straight.

Which leads us to . . .

Case Study: Hillary's Emails

You know which major media outlet first put her email "scandal" in the public's consciousness, don't you? Guess.

"Rupert Murdoch's *New York Post*?" Nope.

"Fox News?" Sorry.

"OK, then it had to be Murdoch's *Wall Street Journal*." Good guess, but wrong.

No, on March 2, 2015, it was none other than that bastion of radical Right propaganda—the *New York Times*. They were the first. For two consecutive days, they put the then unknown story on their front page. And naturally, every other media outlet jumped on it.

For the next three years, you could not find a Republican capable of spouting three consecutive sentences without hearing about Hillary's emails. And Benghazi, of course! Don't forget Benghazi!

So the public bought into the story. Hillary surely did *something* bad—just as with Benghazi, they were always a bit fuzzy about the details—with her emails, and she and every Democrat were all conspiratorial miscreants who could never be trusted.

And that's the end of the story—for Republicans and many others as well. Except it's not.

On June 14, 2018, the Department of Justice's Office of the Inspector General released its report on the FBI's and DOJ's handling of the Clinton email investigation. They found no evidence of political bias in the investigations, and they supported the decision to not prosecute Ms. Clinton.

Much more important, however, was the conclusion of a three-year State Department investigation. It said in September 2019, with Trump in the White House and Republicans running the Senate, that they found "no persuasive evidence

of systemic, deliberate mishandling of classified information."*
The State Department report was a complete repudiation of
the main tenets of the Clinton email "scandal."

And lo and behold, Hillary's exoneration was front-page
news in every newspaper. Fox News issues an apology! Even
Rush Limbaugh . . . oh, wait. None of that happened.

The *New York Times*, being the newspaper of record, duti-
fully reported on the exoneration but buried it deep within
the main section. And none of the other major news organizations gave it much more visibility—if they covered it at all.

So the stain on the Democratic standard-bearer of 2016,
our first major-party female presidential candidate, remains
permanently etched in the minds of voters in every precinct.
And once again, Democrats failed to aggressively work to
wash that stain away.

Whether it's Benghazi or "her emails," Republicans won
the branding war.

Even if voters didn't know the details of either so-called
scandal, even if the truth and facts were not what they believed,
voters still had the *feeling* there was something "shady" about
Hillary Clinton. *And that's how branding works.* It's the feeling

---

* Mary C. Jalonick and Matthew Lee, "38 People Cited for Violations in Clinton Email Probe," Associated Press, October 19, 2019, https://apnews.com/
article/email-clinton-classified-information-chuck-grassley-politics-14b14afc-
5d8647858489a2cf5385c28d.

Republican politicians created that stayed with many people and influenced how they voted.

All this again begs the question: Why don't Democrats have a centralized, active, well-funded group ready to counter Republican propaganda?

Turn Republicans' Own Words against Them

Here's the typical claptrap we heard during the 2020 Republican campaign, spewed from the former president on down.

- Democrats are socialists! Communists even!
- The suburbs will be destroyed!
- The borders will be wide open! Rapists and thieves and drug addicts will come pouring in!
- Democrats are coming for your guns!
- Antifa and Black Lives Matter will burn your cities!
- They will close your churches, and the schools will indoctrinate your children!
- Freedom will be lost forever!
- Violent gangs will roam the streets!
- Your 401(k) will be wiped out!

All these and more were recurring themes in the 2020 election. And it continues today.

It's all nonsense, of course, but millions believed—and continue to believe—all of it. We can and should bludgeon Republicans with their own words. These lies must be countered forcefully and continually.

Don't let them get away with brainwashing America using false fears. How? By being prepared at all times to give clear, forceful, factual rebuttals.

Candidates should throw those lies and crackpot theories back in the faces of their GOP opponents. Stop letting them get away with lying about who we are. Or lying about reality.

For example . . .

Mock Republicans' "Socialist" Whining

Cuba! Venezuela! Gulags!

Socialism!

Republicans toss that word around like dollar bills at a strip club. Ronald Reagan, all the way back when he was still a B-list actor, gave a speech warning the nation of the "horrors of socialism that would befall us under Medicare."

Ha! Ask the millions of senior citizens if they are ready to burn their Medicare cards to sidestep the "horrors" of the system that ensures they have decent health care.

In fact, all the way back in 1952, President Harry Truman pointed out that "socialism" was the knee-jerk response of

Republicans to New Deal policies. He said it became "a scare word they have hurled at every advance the people have made in the last twenty years."*

He listed New Deal policies—Social Security, the FDIC, price supports for farmers, public power systems, and labor rights—as examples that Republicans had denounced as "creeping socialism."

Truman correctly said, "Socialism is their name for almost anything that helps all the people."†

Yes! That's a brilliant and powerful rejoinder to the "socialism" charge. Use it.

It's the same with open borders, defund the police, nanny state, and all the other scornful phrases they hurl at our candidates. Get the facts, and then mock the way Republicans fall back on simplistic phrases in place of thoughtful policy discussions.

Feel free to say, when appropriate, "Stop your whining. Let's deal with this like grown-ups."

---

* Harry Truman, "Rear Platform and Other Informal Remarks in New York" (speech, New York, October 10, 1952) Harry S. Truman Presidential Library and Museum, https://www.trumanlibrary.gov/library/public-papers/289/rear-platform-and-other-informal-remarks-new-york.

† Ibid.

A Day in the Life of a Socialist

The following has been floating around the internet for some time. It's attributed to someone named Kay Dee, which we assume is a pseudonym. There is nothing here that you don't know already, but seeing it in this hypothetical story line helps humanize the absurdity of Republican fear-mongering about "socialism."

Additionally, it could provide good fodder for Democrats who need to soften or personalize their reliance on hard facts.

A Day in the Life of Sue, a Trump Supporter

Sue gets up at 6:00 a.m. and fills her coffeepot with water to prepare her morning coffee. The water is clean and good because some tree-hugging liberal fought for minimum water-quality standards.

With her first swallow of coffee, she takes her daily medication. Her medications are safe to take because some stupid commie liberal fought to ensure their safety and that they work as advertised.

All but ten dollars of her medications are paid for by her employer's medical plan because some liberal union workers fought their employers for paid medical insurance; now Sue gets it too.

She prepares her morning breakfast: bacon and eggs. Sue's

bacon is safe to eat because some girly-man liberal fought for laws to regulate the meatpacking industry.

In the shower, Sue reaches for her shampoo. Her bottle is properly labeled with each ingredient and its amount in the total contents because some crybaby liberal fought for her right to know what she was putting on her body and how much it contained.

Sue dresses, walks outside, and takes a deep breath. The air she breathes is clean because some environmentalist wacko liberal fought for laws to stop industries from polluting our air.

She walks to the subway station for her government-subsidized ride to work. It saves her considerable money in parking and transportation fees because some fancy-pants liberal fought for affordable public transportation, which gives everyone the opportunity to be a contributor.

Sue begins her workday. She has a good job with excellent pay, medical benefits, retirement, paid holidays, and vacation because some lazy liberal union members fought and died for these working standards. Sue's employer pays these standards because Sue's employer doesn't want his employees to call the union.

If Sue is hurt on the job or becomes unemployed, she'll get a worker compensation or unemployment check because some stupid liberal didn't think she should lose her home because of her temporary misfortune.

It's noon, and Sue needs to make a bank deposit so she can pay some bills. Sue's deposit is federally insured by the FSLIC because some godless liberal wanted to protect Sue's money from unscrupulous bankers who ruined the banking system before the Great Depression.

Sue has to pay her Fannie Mae–underwritten mortgage and her below-market federal student loan because some elitist liberal decided Sue and the government would be better off if she was educated and earned more money over her lifetime.

Sue is home from work. She plans to visit her father this evening at his farm home in the country. She gets in her car for the drive. Her car is among the safest in the world because some America-hating liberal fought for car safety standards.

She arrives at her childhood home. Her generation was the third to live in the house financed by Farmers' Home Administration because bankers didn't want to make rural loans. The house didn't have electricity until some big-government liberal stuck his nose where it didn't belong and demanded rural electrification.

She is happy to see her father, who is now retired. Her father lives on Social Security and a union pension because some wine-drinking, cheese-eating liberal made sure he could take care of himself so Sue wouldn't have to.

Sue gets back in her car for the ride home and turns on a radio talk show. The radio host keeps saying that liberals are bad and conservatives are good. He doesn't mention that Republicans have fought against every protection and benefit Sue enjoys throughout her day. Sue agrees: "We don't need those big-government liberals ruining our lives! After all, I'm self-made and believe everyone should take care of themselves, just like I have."

Everything in this satire rings true, and much of it can be the basis for gentle—or not-so-gentle—retorts when confronted with accusations of raging socialism.

Highlight the Sliminess of Republican Candidates

Certainly not all Democratic politicians are saints. But simply put, Republicans seem to have a lower integrity bar than we do. Perhaps it's the Limbaugh-Trump effect: Truth is optional. Moral values apply only when convenient.

Donald Trump was the slimiest candidate of all. For the only time in US history, we had a president with *no* redeeming qualities—nothing you'd want your children to emulate. Specifically:

He has no **empathy or compassion** for other humans. After any significant tragedy, he could only deliver words of comfort if they were written for him.

He's not **intellectually curious**. Apparently, he reads no books or newspapers. He didn't even read the vital reports from his staff or from US intelligence agencies.

There is no evidence of a true **sense of humor**.

He is a nonstop **pathological liar**, as documented by fact-checkers around the world, his own niece (a psychologist), and his sister (as heard in leaked recordings).

He has no sense of **shame or embarrassment**. Paying hush money to porn stars, suffering through multiple bankruptcies, or being caught in thousands of lies means nothing to him.

He was a **remote, uncaring parent** and grandparent. Unlike every other president in modern times, there are no scenes of family play or simply enjoying each other's company.

He has no **connection to any art**, performing or otherwise, which is why he was the only president who never attended any of the Kennedy Center Honors.

He has no respect for American **history or historical norms**. Anything that doesn't benefit him is ignored or belittled.

Loyalty? That's been shown myriad times only to flow to him, **never from him**.

Business smarts? No, he's definitely not the great business leader he wants us to believe. He squandered much of the fortune he inherited from his father, and he's bungled or bankrupted virtually everything he's tried on his own.

Ethics? He cheats on his spouses and his business

connections with equal disdain. The Trump Foundation was forced to shut down after being accused by the New York attorney general of a "shocking pattern of illegality."*

Charity? Despite proclaiming great wealth, he has given only grudgingly and sparingly. Reporters struggle to find any significant no-strings-attached gifts to any person, group, or institution.

What we do know with certainty is that he is a master con artist, a grifter who takes but never gives. And sadly, he took America down with him.

Plus, in addition to all his personal failings, Trump:

- Has been impeached, once before and once after the election;
- Paid a $25 million fine for fraud connected to Trump University;
- Was accused of sexual assault by dozens of women;
- Bankrupted many businesses; and
- Blew up the national debt by an additional trillion dollars *before* the pandemic hit.

---

* New York State Office of the Attorney General, "A.G. Underwood Announces Stipulation Dissolving Trump Foundation Under Judicial Supervision, With AG Review Of Recipient Charities," news release, December 18, 2018, Office of the Attorney General, https://ag.ny.gov/press-release/2018/ag-underwood-announces-stipulation-dissolving-trump-foundation-under-judicial.

By any normal yardstick, he is a despicable human being. Yet he managed to get just about all Evangelical Christians into his camp, and Joe Biden won key swing states by only narrow margins!

This is nuts. This is like bad fiction.

Again, all this points to Democrats failing to "sell" our ideas and values. Trump should have been a sitting duck for our side. But he wasn't.

There are so many others in the slimy GOP camp—or more accurately, cult—aside from Donald Trump. There are the QAnon believers, the overt or barely undercover racists, the morally ambiguous, and the just plain dumb and obnoxious.

Here's an off-the-cuff rogues list: Ted Cruz, Matt Gaetz, Marjorie Taylor Greene, Tom Cotton, Lindsey Graham, Rand Paul, Jim Jordan, Louie Gohmert, Paul Gosar, Devin Nunes, and Lauren Boebert.

Each of them has said and done things that are nutty, seditious, or dangerous—with virtually zero pushback from their Republican colleagues.

They all should feel the burning spotlight of our scrutiny.

If Democrats don't call them out, who will? Since the media won't, we need to do the negative branding.

Tie Republicans to the "Worst President Ever"

His Reign of Error began when he insisted, falsely, that his inaugural crowd was the biggest ever, and it ended—sort of—when he incited the January 6 insurrection.

For all the damage Donald Trump foisted upon America, the silver lining is that we now have a mountain of a target. And being that 147 congressional Republicans voted, *at Trump's behest*, to overturn Joe Biden's election, they deserve to be forever tarred with that deeply seditious act.

Never forget the Trump legacy:

- He rose to political prominence by promoting the racist and contemptible "birther" lie about Barack Obama. He claimed that he sent a team of investigators to Hawaii to check, "and they cannot believe what they're finding." They found nothing because there was no such team.
- He left the economy in shambles.
- During the COVID-19 pandemic, many thousands of Americans died needlessly because of his stubbornness (he rarely wore a mask in public), his ignorance, and his disparaging of science.
- He eroded trust in just about every government agency and caused Americans to lose faith in the free press.

- For his own political gain he vigorously promoted dis-unity—"LIBERATE MICHIGAN!" he tweeted when the governor called for a life-saving mask mandate. That was one of thousands of examples.
- He continually tried to use his office for personal financial gain.
- He never conceded his loss to Joe Biden. Instead, he foisted the Big Lie upon the public, claiming, with no evidence, that there had been widespread fraud.
- He incited the insurrection that stormed the Capitol on January 6.
- He was the only president to be impeached twice.

He said he knew "the best people," but surrounded himself with a rogues' gallery of misfits:

- **Michael Flynn**, Trump's first national security advisor, **pled guilty** to lying to the FBI.
- **Paul Manafort**, longtime Republican Party campaign consultant and former chairman of the Trump presidential campaign, was **convicted** of tax and bank fraud.
- **Roger Stone**, Trump's confidant and longtime friend, was **sentenced to prison** for forty months.
- **Steve Bannon**, Trump's political guru and onetime chief strategist, was **charged with defrauding donors**

of hundreds of thousands of dollars in a border wall fundraising campaign.

- **Michael Cohen**, Trump's personal attorney for ten years, was **jailed for fraud, tax evasion, lying to Congress, and campaign finance violations** related to making hush money payments to women to keep quiet allegations Trump engaged in extramarital affairs.
- **Rick Gates**, onetime deputy campaign chairman for Trump, was **convicted** for helping Manafort conceal $75 million in foreign bank accounts from their years of Ukraine lobbying work.

And postpresidency, we can assume from the July 1, 2021, **indictment** of Allen Weisselberg, the chief financial officer of The Trump Organization, that his lauded businesses were rife with shady business practices. New Yorkers have known or suspected that for years.

Trump's "personal lawyer," **Rudy Giuliani**, had his license to practice law in New York **suspended** in a ruling that cited his "false and misleading statements" about Trump's election loss. Thirteen days later, it was also suspended in Washington, DC.

Tom Barrack, Trump's close ally and chairman of the inaugural committee, was **arrested and charged** with illegal foreign lobbying on behalf of the United Arab Emirates and also charged with obstruction of justice and making false statements to federal law enforcement agents.

Those are just the scoundrels in Trump's immediate circle. Take one step further out of that close-up orbit, and the number grows exponentially.

Instead of draining the swamp, Trump foisted on us the swampiest administration in modern history. And unlike any other major politician, Trump had an astounding list of close associates who turned on him, including:

- **Tony Schwartz**, ghostwriter of Trump's book, *The Art of the Deal*, said many times that Trump is a dangerous psychopath.
- **Barbara Res**, former executive vice president at the Trump Organization, said, "I knew he was ill for the last thirty-five years."* She worked hard to defeat him.
- **Anthony Scaramucci**, former White House communications director, fired after eleven days and worked to defeat Trump. He said Trump was a "cunning sociopath."†

---

* Barbara Res, "Ex-Trump Executive: I Knew He Was Ill for Last 35 Years," *New York Daily News*, January 30, 2017, https://www.nydailynews.com/opinion/ex-trump-executive-knew-ill-35-years-article-1.2959293.

† "Downfall," The Trump Show (British Broadcasting Corporation, January 19, 2021), https://www.bbc.co.uk/programmes/p093rzhd.

- **General Jim Mattis**, his former defense secretary, quit the administration and wrote an article that included this scathing line: "We are witnessing the consequences of three years without mature leadership."[*]
- **Mary Trump**, his niece and a clinical psychologist, said repeatedly that her uncle cannot be trusted about anything. She warned he was "criminal, cruel, and traitorous."[†]

For those and many other reasons, there is no doubt he will go down as the *worst president ever*. Now we must *brand* him with that label. We must sell that as a fact.

The worst president ever. *The worst president ever.* We need to say that now and for years into the future. We need to say it verbally and in our political ads. Over and over. Make it permeate the American mind. Make it a fact.

It *is* a fact.

Make it known to all voters, but especially to younger and newer voters. In the same way that many begrudgingly accept

---

[*] James Mattis, "In Union There Is Strength," *Atlantic*, June 3, 2020, https://www.theatlantic.com/politics/archive/2020/06/james-mattis-denounces-trump-protests-militarization/612640/.

[†] Michael R Sisak, "Niece says 'cruel and traitorous' Trump belongs in prison," *AP News* (blog), Associated Press, December 4, 2020, https://apnews.com/article/mary-trump-donald-trump-cruel-traitorous-c2c6812cdc5e1daeaf-111d566e52f405.

that Tom Brady is the best quarterback ever, we must make it known and accepted by all that the twice-impeached, anti-facts, anti-science, and anti–American values former president is the worst president ever. Period. No debate.

And then we tie every Republican candidate to Donald Trump. They groveled before him and they must now reap what they've sown.

Just as they tried to tie Joe Biden and all Democrats to the most "radical" defund-the-police elements of the party, and made millions believe that Democrats are Venezuela-loving socialists, we must turn the tables on them. With fervor. With constant repetition. With conviction.

The words *worst president ever* should flow off the tongue of every Democrat, at every opportunity, whenever speaking about that former president. He is no longer "The Donald." He should not be referred to simply as "former president Trump."

No. He is the worst president ever. No one should wonder to whom you refer when you say those words.

Joe Biden called him that during the debates. You should too.

When talking about the former president, freely use descriptors like "grifter," "con artist," and "corrupt." Don't hold back. This is a monumentally important *branding* exercise.

Our attitude toward Republicans, especially those who supported his Big Lie, ought to be, "You wanted him. You got him."

Go on Fox News

For years we were adamantly opposed to Democrats going on Fox News. No longer. Republicans want to paint you as socialists to the left of Venezuela or Cuba or any other failed state. Or they'll hint that you're actually a Communist who's happy to make America a carbon copy of China during its worst Cultural Revolution period.

That's nonsense, of course, but millions of Americans believe it. They believe that and much more, and much worse. The QAnon crazies are just one slice of what used to be the radical Right but now passes as mainstream Republican.

A Reuters/Ipsos poll, released April 2, 2021, says an astonishing 55 percent of Republicans believe Trump's 2020 election loss resulted from illegal voting or election rigging. And 35 percent of Republicans agreed that the people who gathered at the Capitol on January 6 were peaceful, law-abiding Americans *and* that it was actually led by violent left-wing protestors trying to make Trump look bad!* That makes no sense, but that's today's GOP.

So we must counter that nuttiness when we can. And the best way to do that is to reach them where they are: at home, watching right-wing media. We can be polite and patient, but

---

* Ipsos, "Reuters/Ipsos: Trumps Coattails (04/02/2021)," news release, Ipsos, April 2, 2021, https://www.ipsos.com/sites/default/files/ct/news/documents/2021-04/topline_write_up_reuters_ipsos_trump_coattails_poll_-_april_02_2021.pdf.

we must not let the lies and conspiracy theories take root any more than they already have.

Again, if we can just peel away a small—even a tiny—fraction of their viewers, it can and will make a difference in tight races.

A perfect case study is what we saw Pete Buttigieg do on Fox News. As an October 15, 2020, article in the *New Yorker* said, "Liberals, even those who had grown tired of his dogged reasonableness, have celebrated each of his three recent appearances on the network as a tour de force and a rout."*

When Mayor Pete—now transportation secretary—visits hostile media, he stays calm, he never takes anything personally, and sticks to the facts without appearing cold or haughty. And at his town hall on Fox, he earned a standing ovation.

Democratic candidates can learn from Pete.

So push your communications people to get you on Fox News. Or OAN. Or Newsmax. Or any right-wing talk radio or podcast. It likely won't be pleasant, but it's worth pursuing the small number of potentially reachable voters in that audience.

Republicans live in their own information bubble. We don't have to accept that. We should fight back as a moral

* Benjamin Wallace-Wells, "The Remarkable Effectiveness of Pete Buttigieg on Fox News," *New Yorker*, October 15, 2020, https://www.newyorker.com/news/our-columnists/the-remarkable-effectiveness-of-pete-buttigieg-on-fox-news.

imperative; those media are killing our democracy.

Counter their lies and propaganda. Call them out for their most egregious, incendiary blather. And be sure you never come across as patronizing or smug. Steer clear of what James Carville calls "faculty lounge jargon." How? Maybe just seek the guidance of the youngest people on your staff!

Or Don't Go on Fox News

On the other hand, if you decide to stay away—and most Democratic candidates either won't want to venture into enemy territory or, more likely, won't ever be invited on to those shows—don't be afraid to call them out. And get specific. Say:

"Fox News spews out hatred and lies."

Say that often. *Say it because it's true.*

Even staid CNN anchor Jim Acosta reached a breaking point. On May 1, 2021, he said, on air, words that once would have been unthinkable when speaking about another "news" organization:

"That tale from the border didn't just border on BS, this was USDA Grade-A bullshit . . . And the [*New York Post*] reporter who wrote the story resigned, claiming she was forced to make it up. But the damage was done, pumped out over the airwaves at the bullshit factory also known as Fox News."*

The Bullshit Factory. Or, if that's too harsh, let's label Fox News as the "BS Factory." *Let's pound that into America's consciousness.* They deserve that title. They earn it daily, hourly. They make a mockery of the term *journalism*.

Know this for sure: Fox News invented Fake News.

Over the years, Fox morphed into a pure political tool, a broadcasting PAC, an arm of the far-right wing of the GOP. With only a few on-air exceptions, they have no right to call themselves a "news" organization.

So mock them. *Saturday Night Live* does it. We all should do it. And using the term the **BS Factory** is great marketing; it's succinct and memorable.

Stand Up for the Free Press

The words *mainstream media*—or simply MSM on right-leaning websites—should never be seen as a pejorative term. We need to turn that perception around.

We admit, and those in the newsrooms will quickly admit, that every report is flawed, as is every reporter. But taken as a whole, the American press gets the job done and is envied around the world. Over time, the mainstream news sources

---

* CNN Newsroom (Cable News Network, May 1, 2021).

give Americans the facts we need to make informed decisions.

Don't let Trump and his cult win on this. America is not America without a vibrant, unshackled press. Defend this cherished institution—one that is protected in the very first Amendment to the Constitution.

Democrats, by the way, should point out that the opposite of *mainstream* is *fringe*! Our society needs less fringe and more serious-minded, analytical mainstream thinking. And mock those who say, as Trump did so many times in so many ways, "Don't believe what you see and what you read." He and his cult followers want voters to only trust one source of information: themselves.

That is the certain path to tyranny.

Please never forget or accept Trump's outrageous statement that the press is "the enemy of the people." Those dangerous words should have provoked an immediate, angry, and vociferous response from the press and from Democrats. But once again, the response was muted and polite.

May we never make that mistake again.

Rupert Murdoch and his clan make billions by keeping their viewers angry about anyone or any group seen as a "leftist"—their term, not ours. Angry, agitated viewers return to Fox News so that they can confirm their biases. And that keeps the ratings up.

Please keep this in mind:

Journalism is a calling. Fox News is a business model.
They should never be confused. The American free press does lean (slightly) left, but only because pro journalists seek truth, not political flimflam.

Chapter 4 Summary

- Build a swift and potent strike force to counter lies and distortions.
- Get to know your opponent.
- Change your vocabulary—old to new.
- Rebrand Republicans as the "radical Right."
- Call extremists what they are: extremists.
- Go on the offense. Push them on dark money, tax inequities, tax cheats, income inequality, and the climate emergency.
- Use Republicans to fight our battles. It's good when we attack Republicans. It's much better when Republicans attack Republicans.
- Make Republicans pay for their actions.
- Label their lies as lies.
- Turn Republicans' own words against them.
- Shine a light on phony trickle-down economics.
- Mock them for their scare-tactic use of *socialism*.
- Highlight the sliminess of their candidates.
- Tie Republicans to the "Worst President Ever."
- Go on right-wing media, if possible.
- Or don't, but then label Fox News and similar outlets as the "BS Factory."
- Defend the free press.

CHAPTER 5

MARCHING ORDERS

Recognize the Urgency:
Start Democratic Brand Building Now

This book can never truly be finished: the hot-button issues we've raised here change with the seasons. And hourly, Fox News will continue to cough up the phlegm of misinformation. But the need for upgrading Democratic Party branding and marketing is now.

Yes, we know that in politics nothing beats "feet on streets." Without a solid ground game, without dedicated, well-funded campaign staffs bolstered by hordes of volunteers, even the most brilliant politician has little hope. That's a given.

But we also know that Democrats don't have time to waste when it comes to developing better campaigning. Republicans are organized, energized, and well funded. And, as we write these words, the majority of Republicans remain slavishly loyal to their cult leader, the former president.

Democrats are baffled: We would like to assume that after supporting the worst president in history, after losing the presidency and both houses of Congress, it might be reasonable to think a bit of humility took hold of the Right. But no, they are doubling down.

Here's one example out of hundreds: On April 19, 2021, Republican senator Rick Scott published a screed on the Fox Business News website. Titled "Dear Woke Corporate America, beware of the backlash that's coming," it oozed with right-wing buzzwords meant to mock, inflame, and distract from actual issues.

Take a look at a sample section:

> It's not that you have twisted the truth; you have rejected the truth. Worse, you do not care what is true.
>
> You give the woke mob concession after concession, hoping to buy time to rake in more cash under your watch. You feed the rabble leftist mob that is shouting that America is racist, hoping they won't come for you.
>
> Amazingly, the woke, liberal corporate news media is just as dishonest as you. They support your lies. And the President of the United States, Joe Biden, shows

you the way. He demonstrates how to lie in public and get away with it.

Let me give you woke corporate leaders a heads-up: Everybody can see the game you are playing. Everybody can see your lies. You are the naked emperor.*

The sheer craziness of his words boggles the mind. We could laugh it off but for two horrendous facts. Rick Scott was one of eight senators to object to the certification of the Electoral College, all based on the Big Lie about voter fraud. Worse, Scott is also the chair of the National Republican Senatorial Committee, the group tasked with electing Republicans to the Senate.

Clearly, he feels no obligation to speak truthfully. Instead, he's happy to do what Trump did daily: live in an alternate universe where up is down and black is white.

When Scott uses words like "rabble leftist mob," he shows us that he, and by extension those he works with, are willing to pull the pin on verbal grenades and throw them at every left-leaning target. That's why the messages of this book are urgent. The battle is well under way, and we are not winning it. We cannot continue to respond passively; we must act now.

---

* Rick Scott, "Sen. Rick Scott: Dear Work Corporate America, Beware of the Backlash That's Coming," Fox Business News, April 9, 2021, https://www.foxbusiness.com/politics/sen-rick-scott-work-corporate-america-backlash.

Go after that fourteen-year-old girl and fifteen-year-old boy. There are millions of them, and they are just two elections away from reaching voting age. They need us for their future, and we need them. Speak to them in their language and on their media. They are our natural allies, and they will turn elections.

Go after the I-don't-care-about-politics crowd. Our core issues affect their lives far more than problems at the border or a trade war with China.

If Not Now, When?

No reader will accept or agree with every suggestion we have offered. But we ask you to consider: What will the Democratic Party look like next year? In two years? In ten years?

Will we still be hanging on by a thread, winning or losing federal, state, and local elections by narrow margins?

That is what is likely to happen if the party mindlessly follows the rambling, incohesive election tactics of the past—the ones that helped get us to this precarious situation.

Or will we recognize that the same finger-lickin'-good branding techniques that sell millions of buckets of fried chicken can effectively persuade millions of voters to vote for the blue team?

We need to change our tactics. We need to do that today. We need to change for the good of America.

What You Can Do to Win the Next Election

If you want to help the Democratic Party implement these strategies to dominate the election landscape for years to come, there are simple steps you can take.

If you're already involved in the Democratic Party, request an opportunity to present these concepts we've presented here to your colleagues.

If you're not involved in the Democratic Party, new volunteers are generally welcomed at the local, state, and sometimes national levels. Contact the Democratic Party in your area to get involved, and then request an opportunity to present this information to the group.

If you need help with your presentation, contact us, and we'll send you a set of speaker's notes. All the key points are carefully laid out so that you can easily glide through them point by point for your colleagues.

If you want additional copies of this book to distribute to your group, you can buy them at bulk rates by contacting us at info@brandingdemocrats.com.

And, of course, you can and should contribute to groups like Move On (moveon.org), Indivisible (indivisible.org), and Run for Something (runforsomething.net). We actually prefer these for our donations, as opposed to giving directly to candidates' campaign organizations, as they seem to be more efficient with the funds they collect. But any donation to any Democrat helps.

Branding Works
Branding Lasts for Decades

Branding sells shoes, cars, and toothpaste. In the long run, it is and always will be more effective than of-the-moment marketing. And if we are in the business of "selling" Democrats—and we are—then we need to take solid steps to rebrand ourselves and our opponents.

We need to accept that campaign-specific *marketing* has limited effectiveness because it targets the short term.

Branding doesn't change from one election to the next. It sticks inside voters' heads. It's what a voter remembers when he or she is inside the voting booth. The hot-button issues will change with the seasons, but branding supersedes the daily headlines.

Branding is never a one-shot, short-term effort.

Branding requires time and repetition of the key points:

- Democrats care about people more than corporations.
- Democrats protect the little guy.
- **"Democrats Fight *for the People*."**

Brand Democrats with the good stuff.

Brand Republicans with the bad stuff.

You're reading this because you believe in the values of the Democratic Party. They are lofty and worthy of our efforts.

Plus, we have truth on our side.

Build the brand!

In too many cases, Democrats lost tight elections that were winnable. Applying the techniques we've outlined here can surely help move one or two percent over to the Democrats' column. That, so often, will be all we need.

We cannot relax. Let's build a new movement in America, with a universal message and the single-minded goal of saving our Democracy.

America's future is at stake.

Build the brand.

BIBLIOGRAPHY

"The American Rescue Plan." The White House. The United States Government, October 8, 2021. https://www.whitehouse.gov/american-rescue-plan/.

Barbaro, Michael. "Americans Don't Trust Her. But Why?" *New York Times*, August 16, 2016. https://www.nytimes.com/2016/08/16/podcasts/hillary-clinton-trust.html.

Burns, Alexander. "Democrats Beat Trump in 2020. Now They're Asking: What Went Wrong?" *New York Times*. February 20, 2021. https://www.nytimes.com/2021/02/20/us/politics/democrats-house-races-trump.html.

Center on Budget and Policy Priorities. "Large Job Growth Unlikely to Follow Tax Cuts for the Rich and Corporations ." *Center on Budget and Policy Priorities* (blog), October 10, 2017. https://www.cbpp.org/research/federal-tax/large-job-growth-unlikely-to-follow-tax-cuts-for-the-rich-and-corporations.

Deloitte. "COVID-19's Impact on US Income Inequality: It's Going to Get Worse before It Get's Better." *Deloitte Insights* (blog), July 23, 2020. https://www2.deloitte.com/content/dam/insights/us/articles/6786_IbtN-COVID-19-and-inequality/DI_IbtN-COVID-19-and-inequality.pdf.

"Downfall." Episode. In *The Trump Show* 1, no. 4. British Broadcasting Corporation, January 19, 2021. https://www.bbc.co.uk/programmes/p093rzhd.

"Episode airing 5/1/2021." Episode. In *CNN Newsroom*. CNN. May 1, 2021.

"Episode airing 12/8/2015." Episode. In *New Day.* CNN. December 8, 2015.

Epstein, Reid J, and Nick Corasaniti. "The Gerrymander Battles Loom, as G.O.P. Looks to Press Its Advantage." *New York Times*. January 31, 2021. https://www.nytimes.com/2021/01/31/us/politics/gerrymander-census-democrats-republicans.html.

Ernsthausen, Jeff, Paul Kiel, and Jesse Eisinger. "The Secret IRS Files: Trove of Never-before-Seen Records Reveal How the Wealthiest Avoid Income Tax." ProPublica, June 8, 2021. https://www.propublica.org/article/the-secret-irs-files-trove-of-never-before-seen-records-reveal-how-the-wealthiest-avoid-income-tax.

Graham, Lindsey. Graham: Trump is a "race-baiting, xenophobic" bigot (2015). Other. CNN, December 2015.

Hall, Ronald. "The US Adoption System Discriminates against Darker-skinned Children." *The Conversation*, February 21, 2019. https://theconversation.com/the-us-adoption-system-discriminates-against-darker-skinned-children-110976.

Hook, Janet. "Democrats Brace for 2022 Elections with 'Little Margin for Error'." *Los Angeles Times*, June 7, 2021. https://www.latimes.com/politics/story/2021-06-07/democrats-brace-for-2022-elections-with-little-margin-for-error

Jalonick, Mary C., and Matthew Lee. "38 People Cited for Violations in Clinton Email Probe." Associated Press, October 19, 2019. https://apnews.com/article/email-clinton-classified-information-chuck-grassley-politics-14b14afc5d8647858489a2cf5385c28d.

Kahn, Chris. "U.S. Voters Want Leader to End Advantage of Rich and Powerful: Reuters/Ipsos Poll." November 8, 2016. Reuters. https://www.reuters.com/article/us-usa-election-poll- mood/u-s-voters-want-leader-to-end-advantage-of-rich-and-powerful-reuters-ipsos-poll-idUSKBN1332NC.

Klein, Ezra. "Democrats, Here's How to Lose in 2022. And Deserve It." *New York Times*, January 21, 2021. https://www.nytimes.com/2021/01/21/opinion/biden-inauguration-democrats.html.

Krugman, Paul. "The Radical Modesty of Biden's Budget." *New York Times*, May 31, 2021. https://www.nytimes.com/2021/05/31/opinion/biden-budget-proposal.html.

Lee, Don. "Trump vs. Obama: Who Has the Better Record on the Economy?." *Los Angeles Times*, October 7, 2020. https://www.latimes.com/politics/story/2020-10-27/trump-vs-obama-who-really-did-better-on-the-economy.

Lee, Matthew, and Mary Claire Jalonick. "38 People Cited for Violations in Clinton Email Probe." *AP News* (blog). Associated Press, October 19, 2019. https://apnews.com/article/email-clinton-classified-information-chuck-grassley-politics-14b14afc5d8647858489a2cf5385c28d.

Legum, Judd. *Popular Information*, July 15, 2021. https://popular.info/p/how-corporations-give-republicans.

Leonhardt, David. "Why Are Republican Presidents So Bad for the Economy?" *New York Times*, February 2, 2021. https://www.nytimes.com/2021/02/02/opinion/sunday/democrats-economy.html.

Linskey, Annie, Tyler Pager, and Jeff Stein. "Biden Wants to Sell the Stimulus. The White House Is Still Figuring out How." *Washington Post*, March 10, 2021. https://www.washingtonpost.com/politics/biden-stimulus-sales-pitch/2021/03/09/71dad6d4-80f9-11eb-9ca6-54e187ee4939_story.html.

Lustgarten, Abrahm. "40 Million People Rely on the Colorado River. It's Drying Up Fast." *New York Times*, August 27, 2021. https://www.nytimes.com/2021/08/27/sunday-review/colorado-river-drying-up.html.

Mattis, James. "In Union There Is Strength." *Atlantic*, June 3, 2020. https://www.theatlantic.com/politics/archive/2020/06/james-mattis-denounces-trump-protests-militarization/612640/.

McCarthy, Kevin. Twitter Post. June 29, 2021. 12:29 PM. https://twitter.com/gopleader/status/1409957285816897537.

New York State Office of the Attorney General. "A.G. Underwood Announces Stipulation Dissolving Trump Foundation Under Judicial Supervision, With AG Review Of Recipient Charities." News release, December 18, 2018. Office of the Attorney General. https://ag.ny.gov/press-release/2018/ag-underwood-announces-stipulation-dissolving-trump-foundation-under-judicial.

Nguyen, Tina. "'Pathological Liar': Ted Cruz Unloads in Epic Rant after Trump Accuses His Father of Helping J.F.K.'s Assassin." *Vanity Fair,* May 3, 2016. https://www.vanityfair.com/news/2016/05/ted-cruz-donald-trump-jfk-liar.

Ocasio-Cortez, Alexandria. "Alexandria Ocasio-Cortez on Biden's Win, House Losses, and What's Next for the Left." Interview by Astead W. Herndon. *New York Times*, November 7, 2020. https://www.nytimes.com/2020/11/07/us/politics/aoc-biden-progressives.html.

OpenSecrets.org. "2020 Election to Cost $14 Billion, Blowing Away Spending Records." OpenSecrets News, October 28, 2020. https://www.opensecrets.org/news/2020/10/cost-of-2020-election-14bil-lion-update/.

Ossoff, Jon. "Jon Ossoff: Lessons for Democrats from the Georgia Election." *Washington Post*, June 26, 2017. https://www.washingtonpost.com/opinions/jon-ossoff-what-democrats-won-in-georgia/2017/06/26/0f097992-5a84-11e7-9fc6-c7ef4bc58d13_story.html.

Parker, Kim, and Ruth Igielnik. "On the Cusp of Adulthood and Facing an Uncertain Future: What We Know About Gen Z So Far." Pew Research Center's Social and Demographic Trends Project. Pew Research Center, May 14, 2020. https://www.pewresearch.org/social-trends/2020/05/14/on-the-cusp-of-adulthood-and-facing-an-uncertain-future-what-we-know-about-gen-z-so-far-2/.

"Party Affiliation." Gallup, December 2020. https://news.gallup.com/poll/15370/party-affiliation.aspx.

Phillips, Amber. "All the Reasons Democrats Say They Did Poorly down Ballot." *Washington Post*, November 14, 2020. https://www.washingtonpost.com/politics/2020/11/14/all-reasons-democrats-say-they-did-poorly-down-ballot/.

Rep. *Americans See Broad Responsibilities for Government; Little Change Since 2019*. Pew Research Center, May 17, 2021. https://www.pewresearch.org/politics/2021/05/17/americans-see-broad-responsibilities-for-government-little-change-since-2019/.

Res, Barbara. "Ex-Trump Executive: I Knew He Was Ill for Last 35 Years." *New York Daily News*, January 30, 2017. https://www.nydailynews. com/opinion/ex-trump-executive-knew-ill-35-years-article-1.2959293.

"Remarks by President Biden in CNN Town Hall with Anderson Cooper." Transcript. In *CNN Presidential Town Hall with Joe Biden*. CNN. Febuary 16, 2021.

"Reuters/Ipsos: Trump's Coattails (04/02/2021)." *Ipsos*, April 2, 2021. Reuters/Ipsos. https://www.ipsos.com/sites/default/files/ct/news/ documents/2021-04/topline_write_up_reuters_ipsos_trump_coat- tails_poll_-_april_02_2021.pdf.

Romney, Mitt. Speech. Utah, Salt Lake City, March 3, 2016. https:// www.washingtonpost.com/news/post-politics/wp/2016/03/03/ mitt-romney-trump-is-a-phony-a-fraud-who-is-playing-the-american- public-for-suckers/.

Rosenberg, Eli. "Jobless Claims Remained at Historic Highs Last Week, as Biden Inherits the Worst Job Market of Any Modern President." *Washington Post*, January 21, 2021. https://www.washingtonpost. com/business/2021/01/21/900000-filed-jobless-claims-last-week- historically-high-level-biden-inherits-worst-job-market-any-modern- president/.

Rossotti, Charles O, Natasha Sarin, and Lawrence H Summers. "Shrink- ing the Tax Gap: A Comprehensive Approach." *Tax Notes Federal*, November 30, 2020.

Rufo, Christopher. Twitter Post. March 15, 2021. 12:17 PM. https:// twitter.com/realchrisrufo/status/1371541044592996352?s=20.

"Run For Something." Run For Something. November 19, 2021. https:// runforsomething.net/.

Scott, Rick. "Sen. Rick Scott: Dear Woke Corporate America, Beware of the Backlash That's Coming." *Fox Business*. Fox News, April 9, 2021. https://www.foxbusiness.com/politics/sen-rick-scott-work-corporate-america-backlash.

Seitz-Wald, Alex, and Benjy Sarlin. "'A Huge Catastrophe': Democrats Grapple with Congressional and State Election Losses." NBC News. NBCUniversal News Group, November 22, 2020. https://www.nbc-news.com/politics/2020-election/huge-catastrophe-democrats-grapple-congressional-state-election-losses-n1248529.

"September 29, 2015." Episode. In *Hannity*. Fox News. September 29, 2015.

Sisak, Michael R. "Niece Says 'Cruel and Traitorous' Trump Belongs in Prison." *AP News* (blog). Associated Press, December 4, 2020. https://apnews.com/article/mary-trump-donald-trump-cruel-traitorous-c2c6812cdc5e1daeaf111d566e52f405.

Sparks, Grace. "The Majority of Americans Tend to Agree with Democrats on Top Issues, Polling Shows." CNN. Cable News Network, April 7, 2019. https://www.cnn.com/2019/04/07/politics/democratic-positions-majority/index.html.

"*Squawk on the Street*—01/20." Episode. In *Squawk on the Street*. CNBC. January 29, 2021.

"Sunday, July 25, 2021." Episode. In *This Week with George Stephanopoulos* 12, no. 30. ABC, July 25, 2021.

Swaim, Barton. "'George Washington' Review: Our Founding Politician." *Wall Street Journal*. February 15, 2021.

Truman, Harry. "Rear Platform and Other Informal Remarks in New York." Harry S. Truman Presidential Library and Museum. Speech, October 10, 1952. https://www.trumanlibrary.gov/library/public-papers/289/rear-platform-and-other-informal-remarks-new-york.

Turnbull, Malcolm. "How a New Deal for Global Taxation Might Save Democracy." *Time*, August 11, 2021. https://time.com/6084170/global-taxation-new-deal/.

Waldman, Michael. *Congress Can Stop the Assault on Voting Rights*. Brennan Center for Justice, March 16, 2021. https://www.brennancenter.org/our-work/analysis-opinion/congress-can-stop-assault-voting-rights.

Wallace-Wells, Benjamin. "The Remarkable Effectiveness of Pete Buttigieg on Fox News." *New Yorker*, October 15, 2020. https://www.newyorker.com/news/our-columnists/the-remarkable-effectiveness-of-pete-buttigieg-on-fox-news.

"Whitehouse Introduces DISCLOSE Act to Restore Americans' Trust in Democracy." *Sheldon Whitehouse—United States Senator for Rhode Island*. U.S. Senate, April 11, 2019. https://www.whitehouse.senate.gov/news/release/whitehouse-introduces-disclose-act-to-restore-americans-trust-in-democracy.

ACKNOWLEDGMENTS

At one point in this book we discussed the importance of getting feedback from people you trust. Even better, from people you admire.

We followed our own advice.

We are fortunate to have friends who are writers, and their comments and insights were invaluable. So a big thank-you to Nathan Coe Marsh, Eric Dittleman, Michael Kent, Joshua Jay, Andy Martin, Ryan Weber, Gene Walden, and Shep Hyken.

Above all, Doug Dyment did the bulk of the editing; he organized the text and nitpicked his way through every line and found needed edits that others missed. Any errors you find are surely last-minute additions that came after he finished his work.

Lastly, Congressman Mark Pocan graciously offered his thoughts early on, and that gave us the impetus to finish the book you now hold.

ABOUT THE AUTHORS

 **Ken Weber** is president of Weber Asset Management, a registered investment advisor firm based in New York. He started the business with no formal training in the financial industry's sales techniques, but within a few years it grew—thanks to branding and marketing—to be among the top ten percent of the industry, based on assets under management.

He is the author of the book *Dear Investor, What the HELL are You Doing?*.

Daryl Weber, Ken's son, is a brand strategist who has worked for some of the biggest brands in the world, including Coca-Cola, Nike, Johnnie Walker, Google, and many others. He was previously global director of creative strategy at The Coca-Cola Company and a strategy director at the brand consultancy Redscout.

Daryl's book, *Brand Seduction: How Neuroscience Can Help Marketers Build Memorable Brands*, has been translated into several languages and has received rave industry reviews.